The Burning
Ashes of Time

In remembrance of our uncle
Charles Frederick Bayliss RN 1909-2004
who travelled to Aden on steamships

P&O Steamship *Ranpura*, off Aden, October 1930
Photograph by Charles F. Bayliss

'It was a time of exploration, an age of confidence.'

The Burning
Ashes of Time

From Steamer Point to Tiger Bay

Patricia Aithie

seren

Seren is the book imprint of
Poetry Wales Press Ltd
57 Nolton Street, Bridgend, CF31 3AE, Wales
www.seren-books.com

ISBN 1-85411-398-400-X

A CIP record for this title is available from
the British Library

The publisher works with the financial assistance of
the Welsh Books Council

Printed in Garamond by Bell &Bain, Glasgow

All maps by Charles Aithie/ffotograff
Cover photographs © Pat Aithie/ffotograff
Front: women of the Hadramaut wearing madhalla straw hats,
described by Freya Stark in February 1935 in *The Coast of Incense*
as 'Welsh High Hats.'
Back: Pier Head, Cardiff Bay

Contents

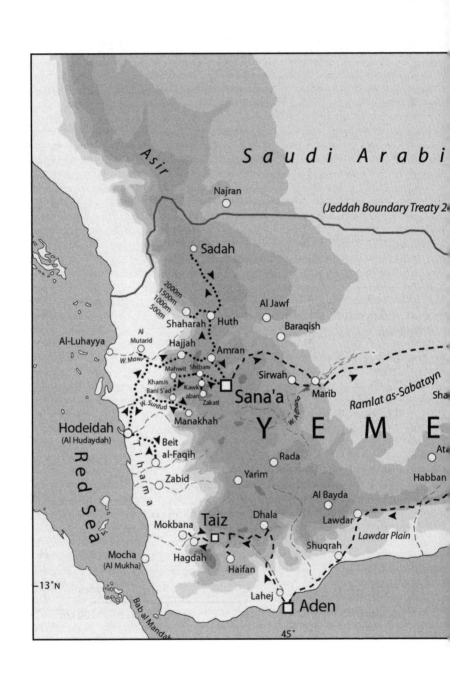

Asir

Saudi Arabi

Najran

(Jeddah Boundary Treaty 2

Sadah

2000m
1500m
1000m
500m

Al Jawf

Shaharah   Huth   Baraqish

Al-Luhayya

Al Mutarid

Hajjah   Amran

W. Mawr

Mahwit   Shibam   Sirwah

Khamis Bani S'ad   Kawk   Marib

W. Surdud   aban

Zakati   **Sana'a**

Manakhah

W. Adhana

Hodeidah
(Al Hudaydah)

Ramlat as-Sabatayn   Sha

Y E M E

Beit al-Faqih

Zabid   Yarim   Rada

Red Sea

Al Bayda   Habban

Tihama   **Taiz**   Dhala   Ata

Mokbana   Lawdar

Lawdar Plain

Mocha
(Al Mukha)   Hagdah   Haifan   Shuqrah

—13°N

Lahej   **Aden**

Bab al-Mandab

45°

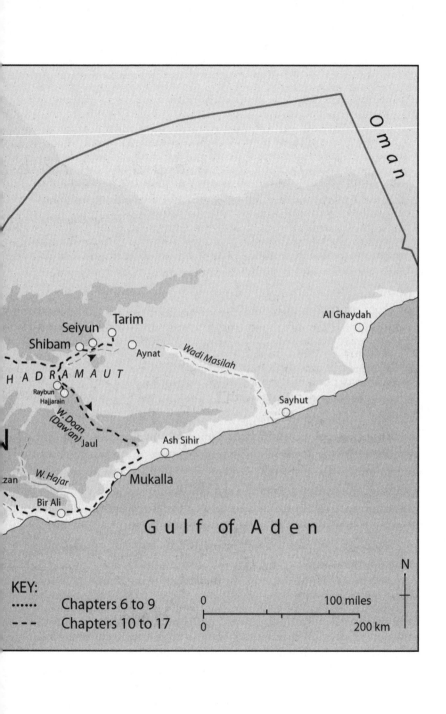

Oman

Al Ghaydah

Tarim

Seiyun

Shibam

Aynat

Wadi Masilah

H A D R A M A U T

Raybun
Hajjarain

Sayhut

W. Doan
(Dawan) Jaul

Ash Sihir

zan

W. Hajar

Mukalla

Bir Ali

G u l f   o f   A d e n

N

KEY:
...... Chapters 6 to 9
- - - Chapters 10 to 17

| 0 | | 100 miles |
| 0 | | 200 km |

Acknowledgements

This journey took place over the summer of 1992 but includes some additional background research made in 1993. I would like to thank the Arts Council of Wales and The Winston Churchill Memorial Trust for funding the initial travel in Yemen for this book. The first visit was made soon after the unification of North and South Yemen. Before the British left the south in 1967, the northern parts of the country were generally known as 'Yemen' while the south was known as 'Aden and the Protectorates.' In all, I have made over six and a half months of continual travel through the regions of Yemen mostly with the help of Yemen's largest independent travel agency, the Universal Touring Company (formerly Universal Travel and Tourism). Particular thanks go to Marco Livadiotti and Mahmoud Shaibani for their generous support. Also for the enthusiasm and kindness we found within the Ministry of Culture and Tourism in Yemen and their interest in my work since we first met in 1983, in Yemen and the Gulf. The enthusiasm shown by the Yemeni Tourism officials based in Abu Dhabi for a public lecture I gave on return from my first visit to Yemen in that year crucially influenced my wish to revisit one day. To all the people in the book who gave generously of their time and knowledge, especially our travelling companions Ahmed Halim and Naji Taher.

Thanks go to Sheikh Said Hassan Ismail, Imam of the Yemeni community in Cardiff, for his encouragement and assistance and for the enthusiasm of many people in the Yemeni community in Wales and beyond. To John Harrison, the Cardiff-based travel writer for reading through the text with encouraging comments, at a poignant moment of decision making. To Mari Griffith and Jonah Jones for being such honest friends in making me reconsider the order and content. My dear friend Nelly Lama, for her generosity and efficiency in translation of some papers from the Arabic and for teaching me how noble and faithful Arab friends can be. To Alan J. Sangster, a friend and songwriter in late 1960s Edinburgh – for suggesting the title and Elaine Williams of Trefriw Woollen Mills for confirming the identity of the Welsh Blanket.

I am grateful for the support of my family and the friends I have made in the Yemeni Community in Britain and particular thanks go to my husband Charles for his caring, steadfast and sure personality which has counted for so much on our travels, and for his drawing of the maps. My construction of sentences, a consequence of the rich mix of Welsh and English heritage, has been a mystery and a challenge for him since the day we met; he has shown much patience.

Finally I would like to thank members of The British-Yemeni Society, British and Yemeni alike, who have encouraged me to study new areas of research and who continue to look for positive and constructive ways to foster friendship between our two countries.

South Wales Islamic Centre, Cardiff

Ash On Their Hands

'People have come to you from Yemen. They are
the most amiable and gentle hearted of men.
Faith is of Yemen, and wisdom is Yemeni.'
                              (The Prophet Mohammed)

Son of a Welsh mother and Yemeni father, Sheikh Said, Imam of
the South Wales Islamic Centre in Cardiff, had just returned
from prayers.

'Ahlan wa sahlan,' he greeted us in Arabic topped up with a large
measure of a Cardiff accent and a broad smile.

He turned up the heater, took off his duffel coat, and peered at us
over the brim of his glasses.

'When I'm in the mosque, with the old Yemeni sailors,' he said,
'I'm hot there and they are saying; Turn up the heat, turn up the heat.
I'm always turning up the temperature, because they were all stokers
in the engine rooms of ships. They cannot stand the cold!'

Unable to further increase the temperature in the back room of the
mosque, Sheikh Said eventually succumbed to the inevitability that his
guests would have to put up with the cold and sat down and relaxed.
We began talking about our bursary from the Welsh Arts Council to
make a photographic expedition to Yemen in 1992 and to research a
television programme. Yemen's great ancient history, the Queen of
Sheba, incense and coffee were all discussed. But our interest was
mainly in Welsh coal which had been bunkered down in Aden.

There was a knock at the door and the dull thud of a bearded
elderly Arab trying to release his fingers from beneath the letter-box
flap. Eager to talk to us about far-away places rather than deal with
the general duties of the day, Sheikh Said gently sent the old man

away, with an upwards gesture of his hands and a few warm Arabic words, that burnt the cold air.

'A lot of people are coming here today. We have an important meeting this afternoon about our new community centre, here in Cardiff,' he said gazing through the window. 'Although we've been here for generations, the oldest Arab community in Britain, it is a new era for us. We've built the new mosque, now we must sort out the community centre.'

The phone rang. Sheikh Said once again switched to Arabic, sharing a joke with someone. He came off the phone with a sparkle in his eyes.

'I recently received a letter from my wife in Yemen. Someone knocked down the wall of our sheep pen and stole one of our sheep. I had to fax the police in Yemen's capital, Sana'a, from Cardiff. Can you imagine? Sana'a is hundreds of miles away from my village, but there seemed to be no problem, they caught the thieves and they are now locked up – it's quicker than here!'

There was another knock at the door. This time Sheikh Said welcomed in two visitors to sit with us.

'This is Abdul Wali and Abdul Rahman, you'll have to speak up, Abdul Wali is deaf and speaks very little English although he has been here in Cardiff since 1922, 70 years ago.'

Abdul Wali sat bolt upright in an Edwardian position, balancing his old hands, scarred by a lifetime of stoking coal, on a well worn walking stick placed in front of him.

The three men exchanged words in Arabic for a couple of minutes, while my husband Charles and I waited.

I asked Sheikh Said to interpret for us, and he sat down next to Abdul Wali and began asking questions about his life for me.

'He's not quite sure when he was born but says it was sometime before the year of the rice and about six years before the Turks invaded Yemen,' said Sheikh Said, laughing over the hiss of Abdul's hearing aid.

It was not unusual for old people in Yemen to say such things. Few know when they were born. A reference to a year when a tree was planted, or a war fought, or a flood came is not uncommon.

'Surely six years before the year of the last Ottoman invasion was impossible,' I said, wanting every minute detail. Surely this was unworthy of serious consideration. The second Turkish occupation began in 1872 which would make Abdul Wali 124 years old. Sheikh Said spoke in Arabic again.

'He swears by it.'

'Then he must be the oldest person in Wales.'

Sheikh Said spoke rapidly then turned his head away from the noisy hearing aid attached to Abdul's old ears and towards me again.

'He says he fought in the First World War.'

Abdul Wali raised his frail voice. His glazed look probably meant cataracts. His hands were wringing the top of his worn stick.

He explained through Sheikh Said how he had been a farmer and shepherd, from a rural region south west of Taiz. These villages were usually inhabited by less than one hundred people who all worked cultivating their own land, usually terraced fields and herding animals.

Following the outbreak of the First World War, in which Ottoman Turkey sided with Germany, Abdul Wali had left his village to fight alongside the Ottomans, and had taken part in battles against the British. But, so he told us, when the tide turned against Turkey (which Welsh-born Lawrence of Arabia had helped to precipitate by blowing up railway lines supplying Turkish forces in Arabia) he swapped sides and 'aimed his catapults' at the Turks.

'Catapults?' I asked surprised.

Sheikh Said asked him to repeat himself.

'Yes, that's what he says,' said Sheikh Said, listening intensely. 'He says he could aim five stones at a man in the time the old guns could be re-loaded and shot.'

Sheikh Said shook his head in amazement. I had a vision of a David against a Goliath. We continued.

'Abdul Wali says he spent the rest of his life on the coal ships, traversing the world, working as a stoker. He says he spent over forty years on the ships routed between Cardiff and Aden. He married a Welsh girl.'

Sheikh Said began listening even more intensely.

'Oh my goodness, he says they used to 'chew', or as he puts it 'taste' coal for its quality, before throwing it on to the fire. If it crumbled in the mouth, its quality was not good enough, and they knew they were in for a hard nights work.'

Quality steam coal was favoured by the Admiralty and Merchant Navy ships, and found in a few precious Welsh mines. It could create great power in the fire and make a ship move at breakneck speed through the most treacherous seas in the world. Bad coal, I was to learn later, was useless and to a Yemeni like throwing flour on to the fire, but good steam coal fuelled the Empire. 'Tasting coal' was not unusual, and later I was told by Dr Nooruddin Fakhri, Deputy Director General of the Port of Aden, that his grandmother ground up Welsh coal to clean and polish her teeth, a tradition in the Welsh Valleys.

Abdul Rahman a youthful seventy-something had been sitting quietly beside Abdul Wali nodding in agreement, as Sheikh Said translated. He sat comfortably inside his thick woollen coat and fur hat. Sheikh Said explained how during the Second World War most Yemenis who arrived in Britain were sent down to Cardiff to be signed on the ships. Other major centres for this included South Shields in the north-east of England, which had strong links with Cardiff. Abdul Rahman showed us his seaman's discharge book, with the place names – Cardiff, Barry, Swansea, Newport, South Shields, Glasgow, Leith, Liverpool, Hull. Born in 1913 Abdul Rahman explained how he had arrived in Britain during the Blitz in the 1940s.

'Churchill die for us to come,' He explained. 'He wanted all Arabs in Yemen to come and fight in the Second World War, against Fascism. I was afraid – all the bombing, boom! boom! We could have been home in Yemen safe in the village – but we were here.'

Abdul Rahman explained how he, like many of these men, were originally brought in to Glasgow and shuttled by train to Cardiff, where all the Yemenis were processed during the war.

'We were tired and hungry and they handed out sandwiches,' he said with a sigh. 'But they were pork – and we were Muslims, and we couldn't eat them. It was terrible and so cold here.'

He described how he was shot at on convoys, shipwrecked in Brazil and saw the retaking of Singapore. As part of his job as a stoker he had to carry ash from inside the ship's engine rooms where he worked, up on deck and throw it overboard. Stokers on steamships became as fit as athletes.

'With no lighted cigarette in the war of course,' he said. 'I tried to smoke once on top of the ship, and the captain was very very angry because of the black-out.'

A crew document dated 1898, printed instructions written on it with the following handwritten note: 'The crews of vessels laden with coal are warned that taking naked lights into, or striking matches in the hold or places below deck is attended by very great danger.'

At the end of the war Abdul Rahman was on one of the first ships to go to Japan and his best friend died as they went ashore.

'The Japanese wanted to burn his body, in their way. We had to start a protest on ship. My friend had to be buried in the true Muslim way.'

Abdul Rahman showed me his seaman's discharge book. In these documents Arabs were often called 'Lascars.' Under 'copy of report of character' were stamped the words 'Very Good.' 'We had to have 'very good' stamped,' said Abdul Rahman. 'If we didn't we would lose the book and ask for a new one! It has been a hard life,' he said wiping his eyes with his handkerchief. 'But now,' he said brightening up 'I have my British pension!'

Abdul Wali and Abdul Rahman left us.

Sheikh Said, Charles and I discussed the afternoon's events.

'They always say it was hard work,' said Sheikh Said, shaking his head. 'But it was a good job to be a stoker. Stokers got good money in a way locals back in Yemen didn't. They supported whole families, even villages. It was a great job to have! They always maintained they were good at their work. Later when people tried to find work in the steel industry, they were asked if they were a good welder, they would say they were the best welder in Yemen. But they had never seen a torch in their life!"

I asked Sheikh Said about his father.

'Yemenis came here at the beginning of the century and fought in the First World War. I am a second generation Yemeni. I was born in 1930 so you can see it was at the beginning of the century. My father used to go to sea and I can remember the war starting and my father saying goodbye to us. He was from the borders between Aden and Dhala, that side of the Yemen. At that time all Yemenis went to sea, it was the only job they could do, they were seamen, and hundreds of them lost their lives at sea, my father was one. In 1939 he went on a steamship, the SS *Stanhope*. It was torpedoed in the Bristol Channel – they didn't get very far. There was not much oil at the time. He was a stoker, he was what you called a donkey man, a little bit above a stoker. He was in charge, and got the steam up, making sure everything was working. I don't know why they were called donkey men but they carried the authority over the other men.'

Sheikh Said was orphaned, like many British and Yemeni children whose fathers served on convoys in the war. He explained he was living in Sheffield, another British centre for Yemenis at the time. When Sheikh Hassan Ismail, the leader of the Yemeni community in Cardiff, visited.

'He used to visit all the cities in those days,' said Sheikh Said. 'He saw me in the mosque and asked about me and they said 'he has just lost his father' and he said 'Do you think his mother would let me take him back to Cardiff to bring him up and teach him Islam?' and they said, 'we don't know we'll go and ask,'

'My mother was Welsh but she wouldn't agree for them to take me to Cardiff in the beginning but the men persuaded her – it would be good for him they said, it would be better. So she said O.K. try it for six months. After six months I stayed and I've been here ever since.'

Sheikh Said moved in his chair. 'Sheikh Hassan rallied the Yemenis in Britain during the war.' said Sheikh Said. 'He rallied them. He didn't just sit about waiting for the bombs to drop! He was even offered a knighthood from King George VI later, but politely refused – he couldn't bow before anyone other than God, not anyone other than God – honest. He went up to Buckingham Palace to shake his hand though,' said Sheikh Said laughing. 'He didn't miss that! He asked the King if he wanted to become a Muslim too – honest! That was the kind of man he was.'

I found it strange that although we have an obsession in Wales about mining, miners and coal, few people had written about where the coal went and how it was used. Yet it was Welsh coal that had been given most of the large contracts with the Royal and Merchant Navy as Britain ran the largest trading Empire in history. Admiralty lists show coal from Merthyr, Rhondda and the Cynon Valleys was favoured for its quality. The swathe of coal seams from Pontypridd to Merthyr were where the best smokeless steam coal on earth was found. Coal mining here goes back to the Roman occupation, and the Medieval monks of Neath Abbey used it for iron making. Yet it was the Industrial Revolution in the nineteenth century and the change from sail to steamships, that drove the need to mine in quantity.

Earlier in October 1775 the customs officer at Cardiff ironically reported; 'We have no coal exported from this port, nor ever shall, as it would be too expensive to bring it down here from the internal part of the country.'

At this time, Merthyr at the head of the Welsh Valleys, had already established an industrial centre by opening four great ironworks between 1759 and 1782. By the early 1800s the Merthyr iron trade, which covered the town with smoke by day and the glare of its furnaces by night, produced over forty percent of Britain's iron. By 1798, for the transhipment of iron, the town was linked with Cardiff Docks by the twenty-six-mile-long Glamorganshire canal; with its 600 foot drop and 50 locks, the beginning of modern Cardiff, and for a time the most successful commercial waterway in Britain. However, up until the 1830s, coal was still regarded as having little use except for its conversion into coke for smelting, and was not for export. In 1801 Cardiff only had about a thousand inhabitants and was a small fishing harbour, its population almost exactly the same as Aden had been before the British arrived.

In that same year the second Marquis of Bute risked his fortune and built in Cardiff the largest walled dock in the world. It was needed: as part of the Severn Estuary, Cardiff bay has one of the largest tidal ranges in the world. To overcome the Severn's tides, which left the bay waterless twice a day, Bute made sure that Victorian engineering would impound water so coal ships could be loaded 24 hours a day. He had become master of the tides. Where Canute failed, Bute succeeded.

The Butes, a Scottish family, had married into the area through the union of Lord Mountstuart and Charlotte, daughter and heiress of Lord Windsor in 1766. The Windsors had acquired their Glamorgan estates in 1704 when Thomas Windsor had married Charlotte Herbert, acquiring the Welsh lands of the Herbert Earls of Pembroke, granted to the family by Henry VII and Edward VI. With it also came Cardiff Castle. The Cardiff Castle Estate, around where I live, was held by the Bute family from 1766 until 1947 and in the mid nineteenth century extended over 22,000 acres of Glamorgan.

The Bute West Dock was built in 1839. This was the same year that Commander Stafford Haines of the Indian Navy occupied Aden by force on behalf of the East India Company, following the breakdown of his negotiations to buy it from Sultan Muhsin of Lahej. Aden was the British Empire's first territorial acquisition since Queen Victoria ascended the throne in 1837. The British needed a coaling station on the new steamship route between Suez and Bombay. They had looked at other possibilities, including the island of Socotra, but Aden's strategic situation at the southern end of the Red Sea and on the route to India, and its superb natural and sheltered harbour made it a compelling choice. The British also wished to pre-empt any move to seize Aden by Egypt's expansionist ruler, Muhammad Ali, who had been extending his influence in the Red Sea and whose forces had landed on the Yemeni coast in 1837. Muhammad Ali's incursion was followed by the arrival of the Ottoman Turks, who established a presence on the coast at Hodeidah in 1849, and by 1872 had penetrated the highlands of northern Yemen, making Sana'a their capital. Ottoman attempts to extend their control southwards into territory which the British in Aden regarded as being within their own sphere of influence caused periodic border tensions, and it was not until 1904 that a line was drawn between British Arabia and Turkish Arabia. However, this did not deter the Turks from advancing south in 1914 and occupying Lahej, only twenty miles distant from Aden, until the end of the war. Following Turkish withdrawal in 1918, Yemen became an independent state but its ruler, the Imam, refused to recognise the Anglo-Turkish border agreement, asserting claims to sovereignty over the whole of south west Arabia. Nevertheless, North Yemen and what became known as South Yemen after British withdrawal from Aden in 1967 remained politically divided until unification of the two states in 1990.

The increased oceanic trade, which relied so heavily upon the steam coal, made ports famous and many expanded throughout the world in the nineteenth century. Cardiff and Aden tripped of the tongues of sailors like twin cities. In fact you didn't need to travel if you lived in these ports – the world came to you. Royal and Merchant Navy ships bunkered Welsh steam coal in Aden, and a multitude of seasoned travellers began disembarking at the Prince of Wales pier in Steamer Point for a day or two. While miners were digging deep underground in Wales, stokers were shovelling coal into the heat of a steamship's furnace. These stokers and sailors came from Britain, of course, but crew lists of Cardiff-registered ships show that they also came from Chile, Venice, Genoa, Trieste, Sardinia, Turkey, Syria, Greece and even the West Indies. But they also came from Suez, Somalia and Yemen. In the hot and humid port of Aden, ships' agents recruited thousands of Arabs to work in the engine rooms, as they could withstand the ferocious heat below deck experienced in the tropics.

* * *

The first recorded commercial sale of the smokeless steam coal used to power these ships came from Mrs Lucy Thomas. A widow, she became known as the 'Mother of the Steam Coal Trade.' Originally she leased the Waun Wyllt colliery, near Abercanaid, with her husband, from the Earl of Plymouth. But a condition of the lease was that no ironworks could be built and no coal sold to any existing factories. Alternative new outlets therefore had to be sought out. Like the wives of owners of small collieries she carried coal in a hand-cart or on the back of a mule to market. Lucy moved to The Graig and supplied households of Merthyr. Working all night to bring out the coal with her son William she put it on a horse-drawn barge bound for Cardiff, and became professionally involved with George Insole, an artisan from Worcester who had opened a shipping office in Cardiff specialising in coal in 1828. After the London Smoke Act came into force, people were looking for better quality coal. Lucy Thomas's was probably the first colliery to be credited with supplying coal to improve smoke levels in London, in 1830. Although these early coal pioneers (unlike entrepreneurs in the metal industry), had little capital, only simple tools and practically no knowledge of geology – Lucy herself was illiterate and is said to have carried samples of coal around in her apron – they did succeed in making surprisingly large amounts of money.

In 1831 George Insole was the first South Wales coal owner to supply the Royal Navy, and started exporting to Malta in the same year. Ten years later The Taff Vale Railway was opened in 1841 to bring coal from the new coalfields of the Cynon Valley, and by 1849 George was sending shipments of coal to Alexandria, Constantinople, and Beirut – and as far afield as South America and Singapore.

In a notice advertising his coal in 1848, Insole reminded potential customers that, 'Welsh steam coal far exceeds that of the North of England in every requisite quality, and to nearly every port, freights are much lower from Wales, particularly foreign.'

By 1854 Cardiff had outstripped Newport and Swansea to become the leading coal port in South Wales. In that year, foreign tonnage surpassed coastal traffic for the first time.

Improving rail links during the 1850s led to the dominance of the Rhondda Valleys in the production of steam coal and cemented Cardiff's position. Yemenis may already have been working on the steamships, but this increased after the opening of the Suez canal in 1869, when ships could repeatedly travel backwards and forwards with coal as shipping lines such as the British P&O Company were able to take the short route east, refuelling at Aden, with its safe anchorage and excellent accommodation. The journey between Bombay and London, which had been previously via the Cape, was shortened by 4,425 miles.

Among the early pioneers of Cardiff's export history were Thomas Powell and John Nixon, important in the early shipment of Aberdare steam coal. Powell Duffryn, (as Thomas Powell's company became) who gave my father his first job as a mine surveyor, started as a Steam Coal Company in 1864 with a shareholding of £500,000. It grew to become the largest coal exporter in the world and largest colliery concern in private hands in Britain. Alone they exported thirty-six million tons of coal in 1938, and by 1947, when the coal industry was nationalised, they owned most of the South Wales collieries.

Coal was also supplied through businesses like Cory Brothers and Company Limited, which was established in Cardiff in 1842 and acquired a colliery in Rhondda in 1869, the year the Suez Canal opened, with a view to opening up coaling stations around the world. Aden was their first overseas enterprise. Cory Brothers operated there initially as the Aden Coal Company, with coaling yards at Hedjuff (the future site of their trading offices), east of Steamer Point and Tawahi. Coal bunkering, as well as providing ships with fresh water and repair facilities, soon became one of the company's most important overseas operations. It later expanded into shipping, with an agency network covering 260 ports, and into general trading. In 1942 Cory's became a subsidiary of Powell Duffryn but retained its corporate identity.

In a letter to W. Stanley Jevons, author of 'The Coal Question,' in 1866 Professor Tyndall said

> It is no new thing for me to affirm in my public lectures that the destiny of this nation is not in the hands of its statesman, but in those of its coal-owners; and that while the orators of St. Stephen's are unconscious of the fact, the very lifeblood of this country is flowing away.

Meanwhile in 1906 Sir Charles McLaren M.P. said;

> The coal fields of Great Britain constitute the greatest source of natural wealth in these islands... our coal supplies are therefore at the root of our whole industrial supremacy... and in Glamorganshire which is the typical centre of the best class of Welsh coal we find the very highest quality of steam fuel... it is the admirable qualities of coal which are unsurpassed if not unequalled in any other of the world's coal fields.

The passage through Aden of increasing numbers of people, following the opening of the Suez Canal, and the seasonal influx of tribesmen from the hinterland to meet the port's growing demand for labour and the desire to seek their fortunes overseas are both factors in the history of Aden's unique relationship with Britain.

Cardiff coal owners also followed the trail eastwards with their newly found wealth. Thomas Powell's son, also a Thomas and a coal owner, sailed down the Red Sea in 1869 for a shooting expedition in Abyssinia. Unfortunately, he and his wife were murdered there, never to see Wales again. Powell's second son Walter died in a ballooning accident and the third, Henry, of too much 'good living'. There was obviously a downside to the excesses of the wealth created by the coal industry.

A Powell Duffryn survey of their overseas organisation written in 1949 states that 'Powell Duffryn staff have a complete knowledge of Middle East countries' habits and trade, through residence in these countries in time of war and peace. Egypt, Aden, The Yemen, Somaliland, Ethiopia and Syria should be especially mentioned.'

Like the port of Aden, Cardiff was also once a small fishing village. Its population increased ninefold between 1851 and 1911 – from 20,000 to 182,000. In the Western world at the time, there was no greater migration and movement of people than those coming to South Wales, except for those emigrating to the United States. The need for a labour force was urgent, not unlike the expanding urban expatriate populations of Arabia since the discovery of oil. The enterprise of Cardiff's 'merchant adventurers' in buying up ships from other parts of Britain (where eighty per cent of the world's shipbuilding took place) had made the city a major ship-owning port by the 1890s, transforming its commercial life. Cardiff's economy boomed during the first decades of the twentieth century when the Empire and the demand for coal were at their height, and the city had developed into the largest coal exporting port in the world.

Welsh Office records indicate a population of 5,000 Arab seamen living here at the turn of the century, mainly in 'Tiger Bay' adjacent to the docks, in the district around Loudoun Square. It was the first major settlement of Muslims in Britain based on seafaring. In these early days other centres also developed, most notably South Shields, but even ships from other UK ports would regularly steam towards Cardiff for its quality steam coal and a change of crew. The coal's high calorific value and low ash content made it the preferred fuel.

The good quality Welsh coal could stand much handling and did not have undue deterioration in prolonged storage in hot climates. By 1914, according to some estimates, the bulk of the world's steamships were fuelled by Welsh steam coal. By the 1920s, 180,000 tons of

British coal were bunkered in Aden each year with most of it coming from Cardiff, with a small top-up from Newport. The volume of Cardiff's coal exports increased fourteen-fold – from 718,000 tons to nearly 10,000,000 tons. Cardiff was the coal metropolis of the world.

It was in Cardiff's Coal Exchange building that the world's first million pound cheque was written, an indication of the great wealth that had accumulated. With the demand for South Wales coal increasing, additional docks were built at Newport, Penarth, Swansea, Port Talbot and Barry, where the competition with Cardiff was massive. The atmosphere in Cardiff at the time was ebullient and its rise as a coal port was meteoric, its exports more or less doubling each decade. To celebrate the success of the port all kinds of projects were undertaken, not least Captain Robert Falcon Scott's final expedition to the Antarctic which left from Bute Dock in the summer of 1910. W.D. Davies, editor of the *Western Mail,* managed to raise a large amount of money for the project by convincing local coal exporters and businessmen to support it. David Lloyd George, then Chancellor of the Exchequer also donated a substantial amount of government money.

The people of Cardiff, conscious of their international links, gave willingly of their expertise and coal to help Scott's ship, the *Terra Nova,* make the long journey south. Cardiff was a boom town and celebrating; its remarkable economic success did not fail to impress foreign visitors, not least those from the Arab world.

In 1937, responsibility for Aden was transferred from British India to London and Aden became a Crown Colony. Since 1929 the RAF had been responsible for Aden's security, providing an important link in the chain of Britain's air communications with the Gulf and India. The Colony had a relatively quiet war despite periodic attacks by Italian aircraft. These did little damage and ceased by 1943 with the collapse of Axis power in Africa and the Mediterranean. Oil had started to supplant coal as fuel for ocean transport in the 1920s, and by the end of the war coal was no longer used on ships. However, Aden maintained its position as a major bunkering port with the construction of the British Petroleum refinery (opened in 1954) at Little Aden. The discovery of oil in the Middle East was a strange reversal of history, leading as it did to Wales's economic decline –

nobody wanted coal anymore. By 1957 Aden was handling so much shipping that it was ranked as the third busiest port in the world after London and New York.

As I grew up in the 1960s my grandparents lived in the Welsh Valleys, a network of derelict industrial buildings, pit heads and coal tips, intersected by Victorian railway lines, canals and terraced housing. At the turn of the century my great grandfather had been a coal leveller in Cardiff's Dockland, Tiger Bay. His responsibility was for the safe storage of coal cargoes in the ships, making sure that gasses could not escape from the hold and explode. Many of the ships he had personally attended to carried their cargoes to Aden.

As a child I was often taken down to Cardiff docks to the seamen's mission by my father, to visit our local Anglican curate who was often found working and socialising there. The main thoroughfare, Bute Street, was lined with Victorian terraced housing whose chimneys still belched out smoke from coal fires. The areas around Pier Head and Mountstuart Square, previously the hub of the coal trade had already decayed. Once thriving with Arab lodging houses, the streets surrounding these business areas were now home to second and third generation families, rehoused in modern blocks.

Our home, (where we were the fourth generation in the same house) was in Cathays Terrace and was full of talk of engineering (winding gear, cables and anchors), coal and shipping. After being a mine surveyor my father moved on to be a lecturer in Engineering at the School of Mines in Treforest. For my father, the world of nature hardly existed, but the world of engineering, ship, canal and bridge building was paramount and his enthusiasm for industry and technology permeated our family. The great British engineers were worshipped and we were taught how their ideas spread meteorically from Britain across the world. At home, in work or on a Gower beach I would help my father carry out experiments with scale models, to discover the holding ability of anchors for his research with Brown Lenox, the greatest maritime chain makers of their age.

Meanwhile each winter evening my mother was to be found on her knees stoking our coal fire and lifting the coal with a poker to allow the air in to create more heat and in the morning clearing the ash out from the grate. With a bucket and shovel she would bring in coal from the bunker outside in the garden. It was a daily ritual. Like many Welsh women of her generation she knew what coal dust could do in the atmosphere – it left an indelible stain on the landscape and the smoke and grime marked everything including the washing. The only time I have experienced anything similar was while living in Arabia, where each week our flat was covered in a layer of fine white sand which had blown in from the desert.

Everyone in Wales knew the true value of coal, the wealth it brought, how it powered the Industrial Revolution, and Empire. Coal sent on trade routes was as precious a substance to the Welsh, as incense had been to the Arabs.

Many ships which off-loaded coal returned with ballast from around the world including Aden, which was used in the foundations of Cardiff's Victorian and Edwardian houses, and of at least one church the 'Ebeneser' in Charles Street. I often sit at night and wonder whether part of Aden is in my home, and how I have been touched by this strong colonial link.

The Old City of Sana'a

Sam's City

'He who blows into the fire either makes flames
or is covered in ash.'

(Old Yemeni saying)

'It was Philby who made Saudi Arabia, and the British who carved
up the Peninsula,' said the student at the Ministry of Culture and
Tourism in Sana'a, the capital of Yemen. 'Before this time, Yemen
owned much of Saudi and the Gulf States and also Oman!' His voice
rose and his index finger fervently tapped the table. His large frame
slumped in the chair as he sliced the air with his right hand.

'All Peninsula Arabs claim descent from Yemenis. Look at Sheikh
Zayed in Abu Dhabi for example!'

I complimented him on his English.

'I speak German and French too,' he smiled. 'Why don't the British
come here for holiday? We get so many Germans, French, Italians...
are you afraid of us?' he asked with a grin so wide that it changed the
shape of his carefully sculpted beard. He stopped talking as quickly as
he had started and looked directly and confidently into our eyes.

Charles replied that few people knew where Yemen was, let alone
had visited it. A look of horror, almost of disbelief spread across the
student's face. To Yemenis like him the country was the centre of the
world, with its strategic coastline, and the cradle of Arab Civilisation.

Ahmed Halim, slim, forty-something and promotions director in
the Ministry, came through the door, dressed not in the traditional
futa (a kilt-like skirt), but a pair of bleached blue jeans, dark reflective
sun glasses and a white shirt.

'Now what can I do for you?' he asked. 'I'm glad you're sitting up
here, otherwise you'll have people coming and bothering you, trying

to practise their English,' he said, glancing sideways at the student.

Charles and I had spoken to Ahmed briefly on the telephone a few days after arriving in Yemen, to explain that we had made no progress in arranging our planned trip.

'A fax was sent to this office from the Yemen Embassy in London some weeks back, and we had obtained an official status visa to photograph for a book and research a television programme,' I said. 'I know that there are still some old seamen alive in the villages who served in the First and Second World Wars on British ships. I want to find them and listen to their stories, and take some photographs, before this forgotten episode in history disappears with them.'

'Really?' said Ahmed, laying his sun glasses on the table. Intelligence showed in his dark, probing eyes.

'Long ago, at the beginning of the twentieth century, Arab lodging houses were established in Butetown, the docks area of Cardiff,' I continued. 'Butetown in those days gave the impression of being a self-contained village and the interdependence and closeness of the Yemeni community in particular was unique. Yemenis often talk about it as if the whole community were one big family.'

'So they ran businesses?' Ahmed asked.

'Yes, Yemeni sailors would generally stay in a lodging house run by British Yemenis, of which there were many. They could mix with their own people, often of their own tribe, and wait for ships to come in with suitable employment, and also eat meat prepared in accordance with Muslim religion. One famous lodging house which also ran a restaurant was called the 'Cairo Cafe' run by Mr Salaman and his Welsh-speaking wife Olive. Olive is still alive. She and Mr Salaman had ten children. She met him in his cafe when she was only sixteen, taking a wrong turning after being dropped off by a bus in central Cardiff.'

Ahmed laughed.

'Years before, Mr Salaman had been orphaned in Yemen and made his way down from Zabid in North Yemen to Aden, where he worked for the Camel Company of the Aden Levies before he arrived in Cardiff. The BBC had made a television programme about them in black and white years ago. Generations of men travelled from Yemen, and lived in South Wales, worked there, married there and worshipped there. Many died there and were buried in Cardiff, which had the first Muslim cemetery in Britain. But unlike so many nationalities that come to Britain many Yemenis want to return home to die. I know there are many of these sailors living here and I want to write about their history, which is so entwined with ours. Yemen and Britain have a shared history. It's about ordinary tales, about people's lives brought together by coal, a simple piece of the earth's crust. It is the forefather of oil. Did you know that seven-eighths of the geological timescale is named after Welsh tribes, mountains and places?'

Ahmed sat back smiling.

Charles turned towards him. 'We have been waiting nearly a week to sort out our travel documents. A further fax was sent last week from Yemen's London Embassy to remind the authorities here. It seems it did not arrive and no one knows about us. We have been sitting glued to the telephone in our hotel trying to resolve the situation,' Charles said. 'We know we need permission to photograph in certain places and do our research. Atiq Sakarib, Director of Public Relations at the Ministry, spoke to us on the telephone and was helpful, but he was busy and suggested we came to the office.'

Ahmed was sorry we had already wasted some days. He looked around the empty office; it was Thursday, pay day and everyone was going home for the weekend. We had already passed by them downstairs huddled into groups waiting for their pay packets.

'It takes ages to get things moving around here,' he said, opening his palms in resignation.

We explained our itinerary.

'We want to travel independently – not part of a tourist group.' I said. 'Our main purpose is photographic, but on our way we would like to look into some of the old British Yemeni connections. Everyone in Britain knows about our ties with India, Hong Kong, East Africa and the rest – but most have forgotten that the British also had a presence in Yemen, and that Aden was Britain's only Arab colony and premier coal bunkering port en route to India.'

Ahmed nodded, 'I know, I grew up in Aden.'

'Ships returning from Aden were packed with Yemenis, and Cardiff still has a thriving Yemeni community, but many returned here. Perhaps we could find and meet some of them?'

'These men live in remote areas of the countryside,' said Ahmed. 'You are right to think you need our help to find them. Visitors to Yemen never go to those places.'

I explained to Ahmed that I had first visited Yemen in 1983 while living in the Gulf. At that time the country had been separated into North and South Yemen ('The Yemen Arab Republic' and the 'Peoples Democratic Republic of Yemen'). There were few tourists and Yemen was not yet an oil producer. We were only able to visit the North, which was still largely medieval.

The Imam's death in 1962 triggered an Egyptian-backed military coup in northern Yemen and the emergence of the Yemen Arab Republic following a seven-year civil war between royalists and republicans. Thereafter the country gradually opened its doors to the outside world. In the south the British tried to contain nationalist agitation with the establishment of a Federation, uniting the conservative and backward sheikhdoms and sultanates of the hinterland with cosmopolitan and prosperous Aden; but they did so against a background of growing domestic and international pressures to quit. Increasing political violence spearheaded by the National Liberation Front led to the collapse of the British-backed Federation and, following Britain's withdrawal in 1967, to the emergence of South Yemen, soon to become a Soviet dependency and the only Marxist-dominated state in the Arab world. Business and trade, which had brought wealth to so many locals (but which had already suffered from the closure of the Suez canal during the Arab-Israeli war) rapidly declined, and many people fled north or to the Gulf to escape the privations of Marxist rule.

Despite the political, economic and social differences which had kept the two Yemens divided, the collapse of the Soviet Union paved the way for their unification in May 1990 as the 'Republic of Yemen'. Weeks later the problems of merging their two different systems were compounded by Iraq's invasion of Kuwait. Because Yemen had refused to join other members of the UN Security Council in condemning the invasion and had instead proposed an 'Arab solution' to the crisis, Saudi Arabia and other Gulf states reacted by expelling Yemeni workers. The enforced return of a million Yemenis and the loss of their remittances (and foreign aid income) was a major blow to Yemen's economy. About a third of all adult Yemeni men had been working in Saudi Arabia and adjacent oil producing countries (as traders, construction workers, taxi drivers and so on) during the 1970s and 1980s. Many now returned to their neglected farms and terraces or swelled the ranks of Yemen's urban unemployed.

'The unification went largely unnoticed in the British Press.' said Charles, 'hardly any coverage, not even a picture of the country.'

'Few foreigners have written or photographed in the region since the British left,' said Ahmed.

It was true. In fact, even when Aden had been a British Colony, the hinterland, or Aden Protectorate, remained a jigsaw of mini-states living in chronic hostility towards one another. It was a sparsely populated land of stony plateaus, rugged mountains, deserts and *wadis* where few Europeans ventured apart from government officials, political officers and the military.

'While on my first journey in 1983, I visited Imam Ahmed's palace, in Taiz.' I said to Ahmed.

'It is now a museum,' he replied.

'Yes, it was like a *Marie Celeste*. The Imam's toothpaste was still in the bathroom, slippers on the floor and in the corner of an upstairs room, a traditional Welsh blanket lay in a cupboard. I knew it was not there by accident as soon as I saw it. Before this first visit to Yemen I had no idea there was any connection between Wales and Arabia, even though I was born and brought up in Cardiff. It was while I was travelling in Yemen that I discovered we had Arabs living in my own home town! When I eventually returned to Cardiff I found that the coal industry was practically dead, but there was a vibrant Yemeni community, who like my family had worked with coal. Practically nobody wants coal anymore,' I sighed.

If Ahmed could get us some practical assistance about the best way to travel we would be grateful. I took out a letter from Sheikh Said, the Imam of the South Wales Islamic Centre.

'We have a letter of introduction.'

Ahmed took the letter and a smile spread across his face as he read the text:

South Wales Islamic Centre

To whom it may concern,

We have written this letter to introduce to you Mr Charles Aithie and his wife Mrs Pat Aithie. They are professional photographers and their plan and aim in Yemen is to research the relationship between Yemeni people and their people in Wales in the past century and the present one.

Since Wales was renowned for its coal mines that were necessary for the movement of the ships, Yemenis emigrated to Wales asking for jobs in ships carrying coal from Wales to Aden. The first city they travelled to was Cardiff the Capital of Wales. Many of them married Welsh women and had children who are now residents of Wales and have built their own mosques and clubs and have succeeded in integrating with the local population without having to melt into Western society or lose their traditions and faith.

So Mr & Mrs Aithie are faithful in their wish to expose the connection of their country with Yemen and seek information from any Yemeni who worked on British ships before WW II. They therefore ask permission from those responsible to take photographs of Hedjuff, Aden, the famous place where stacks of coal were stored at that time.

We ask for the mercy and gentleness of the authorities to assist them in their research and remove any obstacles they might face. On behalf of them we offer thanks for any help you can offer them.

The introducer,
Said Hassan Ismail
The Imam of the Centre.

Ahmed looked up, 'I will do whatever I can do to help you.'

He suggested we write a letter, including a list of the places that we wanted to visit, and he would get it translated and give it to the 'Chief of Tourism' to be cleared.

He continued; 'I left a mountain village just over the border in North Yemen when I was very small, my God, was I small. My grandfather and uncle ran a business in Crater, in the heart of Aden. They were wholesalers and retailers who traded with East Africa, Djibouti. I will never forget it. In those days it was every child's dream to go to Aden. It was in our mind like a paradise, and when I got there I realised it was paradise. It was night when I arrived, and there were so many lights – of course it was electricity – and I asked the man who brought me down from the village 'Are these stars hanging all over?' There were so many lights you would not believe it. In the village there was no light, only the old oil lamps. I was only five.'

'When was this?' asked Charles.

'It was 1952, and this was something fantastic. There were people in Aden with all kinds of languages and from all countries speaking Arabic, English, Hindi, Somali, Ethiopian. There was law and order when the British were there, life was well planned – working, producing. Aden kept its own character as a mixture of society. The British administration was well done. Your history is our history too, we have a shared history.'

'Most people in Britain have heard of Aden,' I ventured.

'Yes, Aden,' he said laughing. 'But where is it? They don't know. Most people couldn't point to it on a map. It's as if it is some mythical place in the middle of the sea!' He glanced at the student, who was mulling over our discussion of Britain's past in the region, and continued, 'The British know Aden, yes, but they have forgotten that now it is part of Yemen.'

'Well' interjected the student. 'The Germans come here and what do they have to do with Yemen's history? I think many Yemenis are sorry that the British do not come here.'

'Many people in Britain do not have the money to travel to Yemen,' I replied.

'Since the British left and the Russians became involved in the South – it has been thirty wasted years,' said Ahmed. 'The place is wrecked I hear, although I haven't seen it yet with my own eyes. I've not been back since 1972. The Russians have packed up and gone. They promised us the moon in our bedroom, but gave us nothing. But now things will change I'm sure.' Ahmed smiled. 'Hopefully things will get better. Leave this with me and come back on Saturday. I will discuss your ideas with some people around here. They are very interesting and you never know. This interests me too very much, I may even be able to accompany you to some of the places.' Ahmed said goodbye and left the building with the step of an enthusiast.

'Yemen was rich in the past,' observed the student wistfully. 'We traded in frankincense and myrrh – expensive products. It was the oil of its time of course, it was highly prized and used in Egypt, and burnt on the altars of Europe. It is true Yemen has a great past! We are proud of who we are, and believe all true Arabs descend from us!'

The precious resins which he mentioned were not only used to gratify gods in temples as far afield as Karnak and Nineveh but also as fragrance in perfumes, and for embalming, healing, and warding off evil spirits. Pliny wrote

> Let us take into account the vast number of funerals that are celebrated throughout the world, and the heaps of odours that are piled up in honour of the bodies of the dead... It is the luxury of man, which is displayed even in the paraphernalia of death, that has rendered Arabia thus happy.

The wealth of the Sabaeans, the oldest and most powerful of Yemen's ancient dynasties became legendary and linked to the alleged visit of the Queen of Sheba (Saba) to King Solomon (who ruled during the tenth century BC) bearing gifts of spices, gold and precious stones. Jews, Christians and Muslims have embraced her in their traditions, and she is one of the few female biblical figures to feature in the writings of all three faiths. If historically she is shrouded in mystery, culturally she is one of the most famous female figures in popular imagination.

But Yemenis trace their history back long before the days of Sheba. According to local folklore, Noah built the Ark in Aden, and his son Shem (Sam ibn Nuh) founded the capital Sana'a, which explains why Sana'a is sometimes called 'Sam's city'. Shem's descendant Qahtan (the Biblical Joktan of Genesis 10.25) is regarded as the father of all South Arabian tribes. A popular Yemeni saying goes, 'When Adam came back to earth he did not recognise it, then he found Yemen'. It is a country hard to miss, being the size of France with a population close on 20 million: the highest indigenous population among the states of the Arabian peninsula, with the richest history.

Apart from the desert to the north adjoining Saudi Arabia and the infamous Empty Quarter, (the Rub'al Khali), much of Yemen consists of a fertile rugged, north-south trending mountain range running more than four hundred miles, containing the Arabian Peninsula's highest summit, Jebel Nabi Shuayb at more than 3,700 metres. In the Highlands, extensive terrace cultivation has developed in a stony environment, dropping down to the dusty humid coastal plain known as the Tihama and the port of Hodeidah and the once famous coffee port of Mocha. Across the desert lies the Hadramaut, one of the world's largest *wadis*, while the extensive southern coastline has been visited by regional seafarers throughout the centuries.

Today Yemen's economic life, apart from oil, is based largely on agriculture, and, unlike the Gulf, in many parts of the country one is more likely to see a camel or a donkey than a Mercedes. Only a generation had passed since Yemeni tribesmen would leave home to travel the seas of the wider world deep in the engine rooms of steamships. But for some reason they had become invisible and unknown, seafaring Bedouin. We knew we were running out of time to try and find anyone who could remember the old days before oil.

Lightning over Sana'a

Lightning Never Strikes Twice

'When a Yemeni builds a house, it is like sculpture.'
(Marco Livadiotti)

We returned to our hotel, the Al-Ikhwa, ('the brothers'), of 1950s vintage, small and insecure by modern standards. The cheap glossy emerald green paint of the reception area was redeemed by a series of photographs of Yemen's greatest sights. There on the wall were images of Sana'a and Shibam, both awarded World Heritage site status for their unique vernacular architecture, and of the spectacular cliff-top mud brick village of Al Hajjarain. Against the background of these images moved homeless Somalis, escaping the civil war. They roamed around the lobby as if they were looking for lost sheep, but their sheep had been stolen along with their culture. These were the lucky ones holding on to what little they had, supported by their Yemeni neighbour, whose generosity in their time of trouble was strikingly evident.

'Your first time in Yemen?' asked the young man at the desk.

'No, I came here ten years ago.' I replied.

'Ten years ago? Where did you go?'

'Sana'a, Al Hajjarah, Zabid, Taiz...'

'Taiz? You went to Taiz ten years ago? You are so lucky. It was beautiful then! Now it is terrible. Broken roads, broken houses, no water. Much of Yemen is still beautiful, but you were lucky to see Taiz then.'

We walked up the two flights of stairs to our room, its striped chintz wallpaper was only subdued by the dull grey paint that coated everything else. The room was hot and airless, so I opened the doors on to the balcony, hoping for a breeze. Instead the din of traffic swelled in the room. The view was poor, we were at the back of the building and a mosquito net barred our view across the balcony, its fine wire mesh defocusing the scene beyond. All that could be seen was the sun trying to penetrate storm clouds, and the tops of a few old dusty buildings.

We needed a vehicle for travelling and took Ahmed Halim's advice to telephone Universal Travel and Tourism, the largest independent travel agent in the Yemen. They would arrange a driver and vehicle for us. It is not easy to travel around Yemen by bus or taxi; they stick to main roads, which would be hopeless for photography. We would be unable to stop where we wanted. We needed to go off on donkey tracks and across the desert, so a guide and four-wheel drive was required.

'There's a storm brewing,' said Charles from the balcony. The sky was an iridescent blue deepening in hue as the clouds crowded in.

Without warning a thunderous flash ripped through the sky, painting it with momentary sparks of lightning, as though the heavens were being welded.

'I'll try to capture it,' Charles said. He picked up his camera bag and a tripod, set up the camera and started to take pictures through the mosquito net on long shutter speeds, hoping to catch each successive burst with the shutter open.

Put off the lights,' he shouted, concerned that the fluorescent light might affect the long exposure.

I sat on the edge of the sagging mattress in the darkness, gazed at the ceiling and wondered what are we doing here? Within seconds the clouds burst and water cascaded down from the hotel roof. It was mid summer, we were in one of the hottest and driest places in the world and it was raining. In fact it was a deluge. When we had arrived the temperature was lower than it had been in Cardiff. Incredibly Yemen has the highest rainfall in the Arabian Peninsula, catching the tail end of monsoon rains coming in from the Indian Ocean. From March or April to October the winds come from the south-west, and two periods of rain are expected – in spring and late summer. Clouds form around the great north-south mountain spine of the country. I could see that at such a height – Sana'a is over 2,000 metres above sea level on a high plateau. Noah's son Shem was right, it was the perfect place to retreat from a flood.

The lightning stopped, and Charles came inside.

'I think I've got a good shot,' he said excitedly. 'Just as the lightning was bursting. Terrific.'

I took a deep breath and fell back lazily on to the bed. It was unusually quiet.

As Charles returned the camera to its bag, voices and footsteps could be heard in the corridor. A shuffling of feet, mixed with muffled voices, became louder and sharper, until they reached our door. A fierce knock came at the door. There was an urgency in the tone, one man's dominant voice demanded attention. A second later there was the rattle of keys. The door opened, and five men edged inside until the door hit the bed end prevented them from fully opening it. We moved towards them to stem the torrent of bodies invading our room. They retreated into the corridor.

An older man with white hair, looked menacing. His hands were resting on his belt which held a *jambia*, or Arabian dagger. Next to him stood another man, thickly set with a broad moustache and a mouth full of qat, a stimulating leaf chewed in these parts. He raised his large bushy eyebrows one at a time, frowned and spoke.

'You have camera?'

'Yes.' replied Charles.

'Give to me.'

'Why?'

'Give me camera.' he repeated louder, getting angrier.

I recognised one of the men from the reception downstairs, he looked nervous and confused, and said to us. 'He wants your camera.'

'Why?'

'You take pictures of building opposite!' said one of the men.

'No. No. I take pictures of lightning. L-i-g-h-t-n-i-n-g! Boom Boom' said Charles in his best pidgin English.

We both stood there waving our hands in the air as if conducting an orchestra. They looked confused and it occurred to me later that we could have been imitating the sound of a bomb or gunfire.

'Are you Americans?' asked the man with the broad moustache.

'No.'

The answer seemed to defuse the stand-off momentarily.

We continued to wave our hands and point to the ceiling, as if it was the sky.

Then I had an idea – I would draw them a picture. I turned back into the room, leaving Charles outside the room to handle the situation. I looked for pen and paper, and returned to the corridor. I scribbled a simple bolt of lightning and handed it to them. One of the men turned it in his hands, as if trying to recognise an Arabic letter. He became frustrated, then impatient, then angry. The man from reception was excessively fidgety.

'Please – Government,' he said rolling his eyes towards them, without moving his head.

They were government officials. What in heaven's name were they doing at our door? But the word government reminded me of something.

Before we left Britain, we had obtained an 'official' stamp in our passports through the Yemeni Ambassador in London. I retreated once more. If four years of arts school training could not convince them that we were innocently photographing the sky, perhaps a few words of Arabic from the Embassy in London would. I handed my passport to the man with the broad moustache.

He stood very still as he read that we were 'guests of the government.' I could sense his heart sinking. He was part of the government and in an Arab country a 'guest' was to be treated with the utmost respect and most importantly, protected. The light caught his eye and his lip began to curl into a smile, revealing a row of qat covered green teeth. His head jerked to the left and spoke the upbeat staccato words 'OK Sorry.' he handed back the passport. But then he followed this with 'Film. Film' – holding out his hand, and moving his fingers quickly.

'Quickly give it to him,' I said to Charles, thinking that at least they wouldn't impound the camera.

There was an exchange in Arabic.

'They will process the film and give it back to you in a few days,' said the receptionist, with a mischievous smile and a faint wave as they sped back down the corridor, as quickly as they had arrived.

We closed the door of our room, nodding to the group of Somalis who had gathered outside the next room and sat on the bed looking at each other.

'What was all that about?' said Charles. We tried to make sense of what had happened and consoled ourselves. 'I'll never get shots like that again, I feel as if I've been robbed. They'll never give those pictures back once they see them – they'll probably use them in their next brochure. I think we should forget the tripod and concentrate on what we do best, photography from a car, preferably at high speed.'

'It doesn't matter,' I said.

After about fifteen minutes we decided to go down and talk to the young man at reception.

'What is that building across from here?' asked Charles

'It is part of the presidential offices,' he replied.

'What?' said Charles.

'They are on a high state of alert at the moment as the president of Germany is visiting, and Germany is one of our most important trading partners. Even the army is on the streets, helicopters in the sky, they don't miss a thing.'

* * *

Ahmed Halim was sitting at his desk.

'I heard about the night before last,' he said with a grin, patting Charles on the back.

'You heard? My God, news travels fast around here,' said Charles.

'Yes it does. Don't worry they are over-sensitive at the moment, with a foreign delegation in the city, it is natural. Sit down and relax. I'll go and find the head of tourism. I want you to meet him.'

We sat down and Ahmed rushed off. Through the door walked a small, slightly built, unshaven man whose trouser bottoms dragged on the ground, covering dusty shoes. I thought he looked like an intellectual, concerned with the problems of life so much so that he was even possibly one that was absent minded. We exchanged greetings with him.

'I have heard of your project,' he said. 'Very good.'

'Where are you from?' I asked.

'Shibam about 30 km from Sana'a.'

'And you work here?' Charles asked.

'Yes, I am in charge of marketing, a new position.'

We spoke about the old Welsh Yemenis and he spoke about the old Yemenis in his village.

'Yes, we too have very old people in Yemen. Often we find they are one hundred years old, they say they were born when this tree was planted or after this battle was fought. In my village we have a number of men who are around one hundred years old,' he continued, 'and, only two months ago one man died who was one hundred and eighteen. He said he lived so long because he did not smoke, he did not chew qat, he ate traditional Yemeni food, no packets, but only what was grown here in the country of Yemen.'

Ahmed returned, amused that the three of us were laughing. He nodded at the man and then turned towards us.

'I've arranged for you to meet the Chairman of Tourism, Abdul Majeed Wahdin, come with me.'

We were guided upstairs, into a room with grand polished wooden furniture and a burnt maroon soft velvet sofa. We shook hands and were offered tea. The manager looked as though he had been transported from the age of ancient kings and soothsayers; aristocratic fine chiselled features, striking dark oval eyes and elegant movements. At times he kept so still and quiet I thought he resembled the finely sculpted features of a Sabaean statue.

Ahmed began by explaining our project, in Arabic. The manager sat still throughout, without even a blink. Then I started to talk, though I was sure Ahmed had fully explained what we wanted to do and I wasn't quite sure what to add.

'Wales,' I began, 'is mostly agricultural, like Yemen, and our port Cardiff was once like Aden.' I told him that Wales was famous for its green land – like that around Ibb and Jiblah in the midland belt of Yemen. 'As a result we have many sheep – about eleven million – more sheep than people.'

Suddenly he moved and laughed uncontrollably and sat back in his chair. Of course many Welsh sheep had been loaded into special areas on coal ships to provide fresh meat for the journey. I wondered if any of these sheep were taken off at Aden and mixed with local herds.

I explained that Wales has an ancient living language, that many people were bilingual speaking English and Welsh, and as a result we had a linguistically creative environment, where even place names are spelt and spoken in different ways. Welsh poetry was some of the oldest in Europe and that I had heard that Yemen had some of the most ancient languages in Arabia.

He seemed very pleased with this, and caught the gist of what I was saying. We spent time discussing the two cultures before he said some words of encouragement to Ahmed and we all rose, shook hands and departed.

At times the Ministry of Tourism in Sana'a felt like a furniture shop; stark rooms containing only scattered plain desks and chairs. However, on our way back to Ahmed's office, we passed a doorway on the first floor. My eyes scanned a room which particularly fascinated me. Crammed with books and journals, papers stuffed into shelves and no space to walk around the tables, it was a shrine to Yemeni tourism and history. In it sat a man in a safari desert suit, a piece of cloth folded over his head.

'Mr Shaibani is the most famous travel journalist in Yemen,' said Ahmed. 'He writes all our literature for the press.' Shaibani made eye contact with us. He looked as though he was deluged by work. 'He looks old but he is only forty eight,' whispered Ahmed.

Raising his voice louder Ahmed continued 'It is because he fought too much for freedom in 1962.' This was the year that North Yemen was declared a Republic, following a military coup against the ruling Mutawakkilite dynasty which claimed descent from the Prophet. They exchanged a few words in Arabic.

'He wants to interview you for the paper,' said Ahmed. 'Is that OK? Then you can interview him too. He will bring a translator.' We agreed to meet at five o'clock in the foyer of the Taj Sheba Hotel, for coffee, *Inshallah* – God willing.

* * *

'You are from Britain?' asked the surprised receptionist.

'Yes.' Charles thought momentarily and then replied. 'We sent coal to Aden and in exchange we got Yemenis.' A loud laugh resounded around the room, as we were ushered away to an upper floor. Here sitting behind a compact desk was another Mr Shaibani, Mahmoud Al-Shaibani, Deputy Tourism Manager for Universal Travel and Tourism.

We once again explained our project.

'The photography is good for Yemen,' Shaibani said. 'but the research into British Yemeni connections interests me most. Yemenis, too, would want to know the story of emigration. It is more interesting than many tourist films made about Yemen, in fact I'd like to know where some of my relatives have gone! They left for Britain and disappeared, we don't know where they are!'

As we were to find out, this was not unusual. Many Yemenis were interested in relatives and compatriots who had travelled.

'What are the costs of hiring a vehicle for us now, and, in the future, for a film crew?' I asked.

'Well the cost of a driver here is the price of a sandwich in London. I know, I have been there, don't worry about that. However for your present trip, you must cover the country, go across the desert,' he urged. 'You cannot go home without doing this, especially if you are going to take photographs. You must meet Marco, the Tourism Manager.'

We were escorted into an adjoining room. Marco was yelling down the telephone to someone about some modern brick buildings, replacing traditional architecture, that he had noticed on his way to work that morning. Marco Livadiotti, was later described to us as a man with the body of an Italian and the blood of a Yemeni.

'Soon we will have nothing for people to see, and come here for,' he said, slamming down the telephone.

He gestured to us to sit down.

'What can I do for you?' he asked, in that kind of cautious voice that had years of experience of seeing foreign travellers trickle through Yemen.

When I began describing how few people in the UK knew about

Yemen, I saw his surprised expression. We discussed our project. He considered the options and agreed to give us a vehicle for 1,500 riyals a day. Ahmed Halim, if he wished, could come with us (Marco offered us free accommodation in a few places where Universal had their own hotels).

Marco explained how he had spent most of his life in Yemen – he was about 35 years old. His father had been a doctor to the last Imam, Imam Ahmed and when the country changed to a Republic his father became the doctor to the new president. The cup bearer moved from one ruler to the next. I was impressed. He explained how Yemen was changing rapidly, how we must capture it with our cameras, before it was too late.

'Every day they destroy something in Sana'a,' he said, looking at once irritated and sad. 'Yet Sana'a's uniqueness has helped it gain World Heritage status. Sana'a has defended itself against centuries of aggressors, but is now destroying itself from within. A cancer is eating away at the heart of this city. Something must be done or Sana'a will die within ten years. Believe me, in the last few years, particularly after the invasion of Kuwait in 1991, when over one million Yemenis returned home, the houses of the old city have been in big big danger. One building per day is at present changing in its appearance, either removing the beautiful old windows, or doors, but more seriously using a new red paste, over the natural brick, which is then plastered with concrete.'

It seemed that Marco was rapidly making himself a force to be reckoned with in the field of conservation, preservation and restoration of the country's unique architecture. I was told later that he had been arrested twice for his attempts to stop demolition ruining Sana'a. Marco was also a custodian of tradition and a man with a personal passion. He explained that he had spent the past ten years restoring his family's nineteenth-century home, in the capital's Turkish quarter; seeking out traditional craftsmen who could work with local materials, at a time when many Yemenis were turning to cheap western substitutes. During the 1970s the population of Sana'a had doubled; fields and farms around the city quickly becoming building sites. His dream was to alert individual house owners in Sana'a to the ancient traditions and living art they had inherited and inhabited and which has vanished from most of the Arabian Peninsula.

'Yemeni houses are built for the human being, for people to live in,' said Marco. 'There is nothing perfect in them, every room, every wall has subtle changes, and has a soul, unlike the artificially manufactured materials of modern houses. When a Yemeni builds a house, it is like sculpture. My house has been a workshop for experiments which have enabled me to understand Yemeni architecture, and start my own personal adventure in restoring old houses and preserving them. I'm always trying to convince locals and foreigners living in the city to restore their homes. One by one, we must all do this. If we don't, soon we will have nothing left.'

'When a Yemeni builds, he builds with the mood of the day,' he continued, 'how they feel that day. And they don't loose any point of light. Where the sun rises and the sun sets, there will be a window letting light in from outside. This means that the white gypsum used to whitewash the house inside, changes daily. In the morning, noon and night, you feel you are in a different house. Soft filtered light seeps through the alabaster windows, like moonlight. Yemeni buildings, when they are empty, are beautiful in themselves; they do not need intense decoration like the Islamic architecture of Morocco. Here simple materials, light and a few rugs, achieve everything. The house is organic.'

In recent years, development in the Arabian Peninsula has mostly been driven largely by oil, which has changed life in the region dramatically and permanently. Towns and cities throughout the Peninsula have been rebuilt with modern materials, using methods and ideas which break with local tradition, diverting peoples interest from the indigenous to the international.

Building materials brought in from the West, can often be unsuitable for a warm climate, by increasing, for example, the need for air conditioning and energy consumption. However, Yemen's more limited petroleum resources have made the country less vulnerable to the impact of oil, and the pattern of life in rural areas still remains largely traditional. In fact tradition has been the guardian of form

'Where are you staying?' he said.

'The Al-Ikhwa.'

'Then leave there tomorrow, you can stay in my new project – Bir Al Azib. It is a house being restored. No one is there at the moment, you can have the place to yourselves. The atmosphere is much better than where you are.'

Ahmed, our Guide

Encounter with a Goddess

'..should Yemen ever be opened up... it will
become a field for the curio-hunter such as had
not been known since the days when the
Egyptian antiquities began to be unearthed.'
(W.B. Harris: *Journey Through Yemen* 1883)

Yemenia Airlines is based in what used to be the only major building in Sana'a to be constructed in an uncompromising modern
western style: reflective glass and steel, in the shape of a tube. Such an
uproar followed its completion that the government ruled that future
new buildings must take into account traditional features of Yemeni
architecture. We were in this modern building visiting Yahia Suwaid,
the General Manager of Yemenia Airways. A few weeks previously, we
had met in London, with Captain Ali Alothary, Area Manager in the
UK, to explain our ideas. He wrote a letter for us to give to Yahia.
After listening to our plans, Yahia introduced us to his marketing
manager Abdullah Mubarez.

Abdullah had lived in Aden for some time under the socialist
government. Then, like so many others, he took his chance and
escaped to North Yemen. Later he went to Cairo to finish school, and
then lived in Czechoslovakia for seven years before moving to Turkey.
We discussed Cardiff"s links to Yemen, and found he knew all about
Yemeni immigrants to the UK.

'My sister lives in Liverpool,' he said. 'My father was one of the
recruiting agents who secured people jobs in Aden during the colonial years. He sent immigrants to the UK, and other places where the
British had colonies, including India. Usually men would receive
their passports in Aden, although there were cases when men went on

49

ships with no papers.'

He described how the sailors were taught to sign their names and how to begin to read and write. To pass the reading test they had to read the newspaper.

'Sometimes Yemenis passed over money and asked what piece of the newspaper are they asking us to read today? Once told they would memorise it, and pretend to read it when they were tested! There were so many people involved it took ages for anything to happen – it is like that now in Yemen, everything takes ages.'

'We know. We've been here for a week, we've only got five more and we still haven't obtained papers to leave the capital,' I said.

'Ah then do you know the story about the American Ambassador?' he said. 'He gave a bull to a village in the countryside, so that it would mate with cows. It arrived and was a big and strong bull and was put in with the cows. Nothing happened. After some time the farmer thought, this was very kind of the Ambassador but the bull is not doing anything. He waited weeks, months and finally decided to go and tell the Ambassador 'What kind of bull did you give me? He does not do anything!' 'OK,' said the Ambassador, 'I'll come and see the bull.' When he arrived on the farm he said to the bull 'What is the matter with you? Why haven't you done what you were sent to do.' The bull looked at the Ambassador and said 'You didn't ask me to do anything, you just asked me to advise.'

It was almost lunchtime when we left by taxi for the Sana'a Sheraton, our next port of call for the morning. We had been told that the Director of Sales at the hotel, Abdul Malik, had connections with the UK, so we wanted to speak with him. Over coffee I mentioned how I had visited Yemen in 1983 with a group of friends from Abu Dhabi, and after returning there had given a lecture on Yemen with the local representative of the Yemen Tourist Ministry.

'My Goodness, yes I remember you all stayed here in the hotel' he said. 'It was newly built.'

Suddenly Abdul Malik's face, which was full of charm, became familiar and I thought back almost ten years to a conversation we had had on the final day of our visit, when he discovered I was from Cardiff, and suggested that if he had known this before hand he would have personally taken me to some unique local places.

'Oh yes Cardiff, I remember now.' he said, relaxing back cheerfully in his chair. 'I also come from Cardiff and Birmingham.'

'Then you know Sheikh Said?' I asked.

'Of course,' came the reply. 'He is a wonderful man, so intelligent, so kind to people.'

We handed him Sheikh Said's letter.

'Oh I have many stories. So many, I can tell you. For example we had thirty men from my region near Taiz who had died in the Second World War. They were all killed together on a ship – bombed by the Germans. The day the news came people from all over the area ran everywhere from village to village – it was a terrible day. Terrible. After that many men in the area tried to make sure that they were spread amongst different ships. Every time we have a big family gathering the old people mention it. They cannot forget.'

I thought of these war veterans, lost at sea, with their families and villages suffering. In the present Abdul Malik was concerned that we should have all the help we needed, and took us into an adjacent room to meet the General Manager, Mr J.S. Parmar, a burly Indian.

'The British do not come here,' said Mr Parmar. 'They go to Egypt, India, but not here – it is expensive. In Egypt and India there are all kinds of hotels – but here only a few, and very few travel organisations. Somehow Yemeni tourism just doesn't seem to trickle down into the brochures. We are having no impact there. If you come with a television crew, you are welcome to stay here – but make it December – October and November are busy months for us, but in December it is better for you anyway – everyone is in their offices working hard so they can go off for Christmas.'

We set off back towards the heart of Sana'a, through streets of random new development at odds with the ordered town planning for which the Yemenis were historically famous. There had been a sandstorm, and as we approached the old town dust devils whirled around the tapering minarets, up into the brooding sky.

* * *

Sana'a's old walled city, perhaps the finest and best preserved in the Islamic world, is sometimes called the 'Venice of the Desert' for its unique architectural heritage. But today, as Marco had explained, the city is under threat from intensive development, and we wanted to document it before it changed beyond recognition.

I have always had an interest in architecture. As a child, I regularly used to walk with my mother past Cardiff's great Civic Centre. The art college which I attended at Canterbury was one of only three art colleges in Britain which had an architectural school attached to it; and, in addition to painting and photographing Canterbury Cathedral, I spent much of my time in the company of architects. In the late 1980s Charles and I were involved in a project to photograph over one hundred churches and cathedrals, and in those buildings, just as in Yemen later, it was the mediaeval craftsmanship and sense of history which drew my attention.

Narrow streets were choked with dust raised by automobiles. We started to take photographs, mentally visualising the image before we directed the camera. It is true that many new cities can be boring with concrete environments where there is nothing of any interest to photograph.

Yemen is home to three World Heritage sites: Sana'a; Zabid on the Red Sea coast of Tihama, and Shibam in Hadramaut with its celebrated mud-brick skyscrapers. The past isolation of these sites – timeless gems in Yemen's architectural treasure house – must largely account for their survival.

In Sana'a the buildings are essentially tower houses that seem to mimic the great mountains around them and are usually built without architects, by extended family members and a master mason working by eye without drawn plans. Yemeni architecture is instinctive and intuitive. Stone or brick tower houses are one of the main characteristics of the country, and have existed since ancient times. Archaeological surveys, including evidence from Shabwa, an ancient capital of Hadramaut, and from Raybun, near the mouth of Wadi Doan, indicate that the use of bricks for building has been in existence for over two millennia. The whole country is like a great treasure chest overflowing with some of the most magnificent examples of building in the world.

The tower house often rises to five or six storeys and is a feature of the landscape wherever one travels in Yemen. In Sana'a houses look out on to streets, unlike many traditional Arab homes which look inwards on to a courtyard. Like their British Elizabethan counterparts, they have their important rooms on the top floor, with commanding views of the neighbourhood. Windows are glazed and topped by fanlights (*qamariyyah*) of coloured glass (an importation from Ottoman Turkey) or occasionally of translucent local alabaster.

In the late afternoon their patterns fall gently across the white-washed walls of the *mafraj*, the reception room where friends and family gather to chew qat. Externally, windows and decorative brickwork are highlighted in a tracery of white gypsum plaster, dribbled with ancient emblems, inscriptions and iconographic symbols from the past – levels of history masterfully and playfully handed down from one generation to the next. At dusk the stained glass fanlights, illuminated from inside, cause the city to resemble a giant cathedral.

Charles and I slipped into the market, or *suq*, through the imposing crenellated gateway of Bab al-Yemen. The din of amplified music from a nearby cassette shop momentarily drowned the raucous cries of street vendors and the noise of local traffic competing for space with donkey carts and surging humanity. The market place seemed to serve as a dumping ground for products from East Asia. We threaded our way past stalls and barrows piled with cheap textiles, gaudy plastics, gleaming aluminium pots and pans, and counterfeit perfumes. A money changer, touting for business, called out to us. Women draped in colourful sitarahs (an outer garment of Indian style cloth) lurked in shadowed doorways, their veils tie-dyed in black, red and white: originally a design for a cloth amulet against the evil eye. Some had circular loaves of freshly baked flat bread (*khubz*) balanced on their heads as they chatted away to passers-by.

We soon found ourselves in a maze of alleyways where the aroma of Mocha coffee competed with the fragrance of myrrh, cloves, saffron, and other spices. Pyramids of almonds, raisins and pistachios alternated with piles of pressed dates and open sacks of grain, flour and other staples. There were shops with leather waterskins; camel bags; delicately woven palm leaf baskets from Sadah; brilliantly striped cloth from the Tihama; and dazzling displays of traditional Yemeni silver jewellery including an abundance of amber and red coral.

The clang of metal heralded an area where blacksmiths were sitting amid cinders, stoking their fires. Through one doorway we glimpsed a shimmer of purple on the wall – a cotton dress of burnished indigo. Until recently many people wore indigo dyed cloth, and the plant was cultivated in various parts of the country before cheaper aniline dyes took hold and captured the market.

Further on, a distinguished-looking patriarch beckoned us into the dark recesses of his shop. In the dim light we could just see the warm tones of pre-Islamic alabaster heads, and terracotta votive animals, tucked away on shelves. Stretching out his umber coloured hands, he unwrapped a soft beige cloth to reveal a bronze mother goddess, garnished with the bluest lapis lazuli. She was finely made about six inches tall and probably stolen from some recently excavated archaeological site. With great reverence he passed her to us, looking over his shoulder, speaking quietly and politely but with an authoritative tone. The goddess was gently cradling her breasts as if to offer milk.

'Where is she from?' I asked

'Marib,' he whispered, looking over his shoulder.

Marib, the capital of the Sabaeans, the Kingdom of Sheba, west of Sana'a still sits buried under silt from the final bursting of one of the wonders of the ancient world, the Marib Dam. It was from here that ancient caravan routes carried incense, used in temples and for medicine. In biblical times the resin was as expensive as gold and made Yemen wealthy and renowned. In Milton's *Paradise Lost* Satan was tempted by the rich aromas of this ancient land.

'We cannot take such a beautiful ancient artefact out of Yemen! It is forbidden,' I said.

'How much is it?' asked Charles.

'120 dollars.'

'That is nothing... for her...' said Charles.

We emerged into the sun and left the goddess in his unsafe hands.

The market continued to snake around corners, unlike so many Arab markets, it was open to the sky. I had been told on my visit to Yemen in 1983, that until the 1960s the entire contents of the central banks reserves for the day, piles of Maria Theresa dollars, were transported through the old city in bags slung across the shoulders of men walking in line, watched by the local merchants. Nearby were open-fronted booths displaying daggers or *jambiyas* for sale. These represent the most important of the forty different crafts traditionally practised in the market. The *jambiya* is worn to show status and wealth and as a badge of masculinity. It is also used as a prop by male dancers performing at marriage celebrations or other community events. Many of the blades are imported from Japan, although some are still made locally. The hilt of a dagger can be fashioned from a variety of materials including ivory, silver, amber, bone and – most highly prized of all – rhinoceros horn.

Daggers vary greatly in value according to their decorative quality and the amount of precious metal, some including gold sovereigns in their ornamentation. Most tribesmen and tribal leaders (*shaikhs*) wear an upright dagger (*asib*) in a curved sheath attached to the centre of their belt, non-tribesmen wear it to the left, while *sayyids* (who claim descent from the Prophet) and *qadhis* (judges versed in Islamic law) wear it to the right.

Sana'a was once home to a Christian cathedral, and locals in the old city still point to a large pit in the ground as the site of 'al-Qalis' (derived from the Greek 'ecclesia'). Some locals declare that Jesus prayed here, in the years before he began his ministry, which gave the cathedral pilgrimage status. It was built around A.D. 537 by Abraha, the Abyssinian Christian general who had earlier invaded and occupied Yemen. The Byzantine Emperor Justinian I, keen to strengthen Christianity in Yemen, sent Abraha craftsmen and materials to assist in the construction and adornment of the cathedral. Today nothing remains, although stones carved with Christian motifs are built into the Great Mosque which is said to have been constructed during the Prophet's lifetime.

This was our next port of call. Through the main doors we could just see a few worshippers sitting on the carpeted floor reading from the Quran. Impressed by their religious devotion, I thought of Sheikh Said who had prayed in the nave of my church in Cardiff earlier that year during a day of Christian/Muslim dialogue. I thought it was appropriate at the time as many believe the word nave (ship or boat) came from a time when boats were upturned to double up as roofs on early village churches. Others suggest the name came from the container for incense which by the twelfth century in England was known by the Latin name *Navis* or *Navicula*. In many Medieval churches it was swung from the church vault, and was so large that it required five to six men to push it, through much of the interior. The Cathedral of Santiago de Compostela still has one.

Highland village

Did They Speak English?

'Before starting consider the end.'
(Old Welsh proverb)

Taha Muhammed, the Commercial Officer of the British Embassy in Sana'a, gently shook our hands and invited us into his office for tea. Above his desk hung a picture of Queen Elizabeth II with her Welsh corgis.

'I've been to Cardiff in the 1950s, and for three days in the 1980s,' said Taha cheerfully in his soft voice. His face was youthful, although he told us later that he was nearing retirement.

'My father worked as a clerk in Aden port for twenty-nine years. He was actually in charge of the desk concerning the clearance of goods, sometimes in Ma'alla and sometimes at Steamer Point. In the early days I was a clerk and shorthand typist, I used to type the addresses on envelopes for an agency that sent men abroad to Britain on the ships. At the age of twenty-one I ran away with my brother, without my father's consent, to Britain, to South Shields and I worked in Yorkshire, Sheffield and London. I had been typing all these addresses of where people were going to, these far away places – so I went to find out myself!' he said, chuckling. He wiped his brow with the back of his hand. 'Because I could not imagine that those poor wretched Yemenis, who could not speak a word of English, could go to Britain and become rich and well dressed; and I said if they can do it, why can't I? I stayed there for six years, and came back in 1960 after the death of my father.'

'So you remember the days when Yemenis used to come down from the mountains to work in Aden?' Charles asked.

'Yes, it is something I can't forget!' Taha replied with emotion. 'These men were often ragged when they came down from the hills. I would look at their feet and think, do they know what Britain is like? They were originally peasants, rather rugged and in not such a good state of health. They would visit the local seaman's agent in the hope of being recruited on to an ocean-going vessel, anchored in Aden harbour. They used to stay for days loitering about and all of a sudden they are in a job. They start by getting rid of their old clothes, polishing up, and disappearing into the sea. They were completely illiterate and knew nothing about the outside world.'

It was true that though many of these Arab seamen claimed to have been born in Aden, most came from the interior in the southern highlands of Yemen and on arriving in the port took Adeni names, claiming that they were born there and were therefore British subjects. As for their dress I was later to see what is possibly the earliest photograph of a Yemeni taken in Britain. It was in the fingerprint and photographic register of the police in the Glamorgan Archives in Cardiff. Dated the 23rd of April 1908 it was a head and shoulders portrait of one Ali Abdul who was imprisoned for one month for stealing a pair of boots and an umbrella! Another reference in the same book, dated the 12th of September 1909, was made to a John Mustapha who looked to be in his late 20s. It was interesting because he was likely to have been the child of a mixed marriage between a Muslim Arab father and local Christian woman. This was an indication that Yemenis had been settling in Cardiff and marrying quite early on in the Victorian rather than Edwardian era. In fact the documents of ships registered in South Wales contain names like Ali, Omar and Mohammed sitting quite comfortably next to old Welsh biblical names like Ebeneser, Moses and Nathaniel.

'Were there many agents in Aden?' I continued.

'No, there were two or three major seamen's agencies who specialised in recruiting for foreign ships. Many Yemenis worked on foreign ships first and later were employed by the British. They usually got information from their contacts in Steamer Point.

'So did they speak English?'

'Oh no. They did not speak a word of English, but there were always people who were on hand to teach them. One man in particular used to teach them English, providing they paid him five shillings for each word taught. That meant that the poor ignorant Yemeni would be sitting listening to the teacher, teaching him words like 'Thank you' 'Good morning' 'Goodbye' 'Very good' 'No' 'Yes' – each word for five shillings. After teaching them ten or twelve words he would say, 'Now you speak English, and that's it!' There was another one, an Indian, who was infamous. No one knows where he is now, but he used to charge for tuition by each word and swindle them!' Taha flung his hands in the air with disbelief. 'He taught them stupid English – things like 'Get out of the way' in an upper class accent, which later did them no good and landed them in trouble! It was worthless to them. Scandalous! Some of the Yemeni agents took advantage of these men. They had to sign a piece of paper to their agent for all the costs incurred. This was witnessed and had to be repaid with commission in their early years abroad and sometimes this was abused. Well one story I heard in Manchester, when someone said something against someone else he said, 'be quiet or I will tell them what you are having for lunch!' This was because he was only eating one potato, saving 70% of his wage for paying back the agent. They would not complain as they needed the work and it would mean a loss of face. He may only be earning seven to ten pounds and he may owe three hundred pounds.'

'So what did the men do on the ships?'

'Let me put it this way. Some of them would work on the ship as ordinary seamen, mostly stokers. Later others would be passengers going to the UK to work in factories. Those who were working on the ship would stay there for years. Of course their English improved and their conditions of living improved, and then they will be sending money home. Those who went to Britain to work would usually be handled by agents in the UK who would look after them and get them jobs, normally in the Midlands – Birmingham, Sheffield, also Cardiff.'

'What happened if they arrived and couldn't speak the language?'

'They would wait sometimes for weeks, dependent on charity. I know one man who had been there for years, who used to take these poor work seekers for a ride – getting them a job and taking ten pounds per head. Just to be sacked after two days by the factory.'

'Did they send money home?'

'They sent money through the seaman's agent who would receive the money in Aden, and then deliver that money to the remote villages. They were called Al Tabbal, meaning 'drummer' or in this case symbolically 'messengers.'

'And were they trustworthy?'

'Do you know how trustworthy these people were?' he said, staring at us. 'They also worked for tens of thousands of North Yemenis who were working in the Port of Aden. Many came from the Midland belt around Taiz and Ibb. The messenger would be travelling first by car to the borders of North Yemen and then on a donkey. The money was carried by about ten people to the villages in the mountains, each one travelling to several villages and that will take him days and weeks sometimes before he returns back to Aden. They were walking banks! They would take a track from Aden to Taiz and go as far as possible. When the road terminated they would pick up a donkey taxi and make their way to the villages in the mountains where there were no roads. In this way money earned abroad reached the women and children in this remote mountain area. In fact in these regions ninety percent of the men left, and so the area was full of women working the terraces.'

'So was he carrying a lot of money with him?'

'Yes of course. All in hard cash.'

'Were they ever robbed?'

'No, the road was safe because the Imam would ruthlessly punish any thieves or hijackers on the road. The peace of the Imam was valued highly.'

'And the men who travelled – did they come home or did they stay abroad?' I asked.

'Some would come home, if they had someone to come home to. If they were married, or their parents were still alive. They would normally return to their villages every two or three years, and spend all their savings, either in building a new house, or on feasts with friends and neighbours. A seaman coming back from the sea to a village is looked upon as a man who should help the poor and give to his relatives.

'In those days the Imam told them that he was directly appointed by God to rule over them. Under the Imam they believed Yemen was the whole world – in time of course this proved not to be the case as men returned, and people would ask 'where have you come from?' They said 'Britain.' 'Where is that, on the moon?' they would ask.' Taha laughed. 'The British were in Aden, under the Imam there was no work, so people naturally went down to the port looking for work and a future. Many emigrated all over the world – India, the USA, Java and Britain. Nowadays men are still leaving this area, but today it is because they want an easy life – or the supposed prospect of one.'

Taha explained how he had returned to Aden in the early 1960s, when the British were still there, and how later he formed his own company during communist rule – even though he did not have communist approval. It was a seaman's employment bureau. Staff visited the incoming ships to enquire if vacancies existed, and then filled them from a long list of people that Taha had waiting.

'Before independence there were two major nationalist movements. The British favoured the National Liberation Front (NLF) not knowing they had a hidden agenda,' he said. 'During the time of the British evacuation from Aden, the Front for the Liberation of South Yemen (FLOSY) lost their way – ran away. Secret dealings with the NLF got them into power, propaganda leaflets had been printed. There were right-wing and left-wing elements and they seized power and then showed their claws, eliminating first the right wing of the organisation and then everything. They say Southern Yemen now has a population of three and a half million, but I'm not sure of these statistics. Many people fled. I saw my opportunity in 1976 and escaped across the border to North Yemen when I was working in the hills.'

In fact within eighteen months of the British departure from Aden the population of the port reduced dramatically.

'The communist way is to get the children to shoot, or tell on parents, and even wives and husbands.' said Taha.

'Did many people disappear?' I asked.

'Of course. When you get freedom, people think they can do anything – but people need some rules.'

'Today things are changing. Presently there is a report on the possibility of a free port in Aden, some consultants did a feasibility study, a free port where the exports are brought in and stored, like a warehouse, and then taken and sold to be exported. Some people are worried that nothing will come of it because of the building work being done near the port of Hodeidah. When the British left, the locals thought Aden would become like Singapore, but it didn't happen, because the communists took over. By the way,' Taha rose out of his chair and reached for a newspaper, 'today Cardiff is mentioned in one of our national newspapers. It says Abdul Rahman, the son of Sheikh Abdullah al-Hakimi died yesterday. Hakimi was one of the nationalist movement figures who participated in the 'Yemen Liberation Society' (Free Yemeni Party) which was formed by Sheikh Zubeiri and Sheikh Noman. He founded the newspaper *Al Salam*, published in Cardiff, that was partly responsible for the 1948 attempt against the Imam.'

'I've never heard of that,' I replied, latching on to what he was saying. Charles looked across at me, astonished that such a newspaper could have been published in Cardiff. It was going to be some weeks before we learnt more about Hakimi.

We returned once more to the centre of Sana'a, and went looking for that essential toilet. We were directed across the 26th September Square (named in remembrance of the revolution) towards the main Post Office. I was taken upstairs. A Somali shuffled past with a trolley of parcels with a young child clinging to his leg. I returned to find Charles with a fistful of qat in his hand.

'The post office clerks just thrust it at me,' he said smiling. 'It tastes like raw pea pods – definitely not for me I'm afraid.'

Qat, *Catha edulis* is a leaf grown in the Highlands and chewed increasingly by many Yemenis. Before 1962 it was used by the elite and soldiers but soon the habit grew and in the northern regions of Yemen it took on great social importance. Much of the agricultural land was taken over, yielding great profits for the growers, and consuming a third of the country's water. Most afternoons the men, (and more and more frequently these days – women) in the north spend time chewing this plant in a party called a *maqil*, or smoking the *mada'ah*, a water pipe. In the south, since unification in 1990, qat is used increasingly. Usually friends gather together, each bringing their own bundle of leaves which they throw on the floor before them. Only the most tender small leaves are chewed and stored in the side of one cheek, wetted occasionally by mineral water, or Coca Cola. Locals see the chewing of qat as a kind of ritual for maintaining or renewing relationships. They believe it gives great stamina, and increases awareness. As qat is chewed, the natural mood of the chewers is enhanced, they exchange news or discuss the days events. Philosophic statements and jokes abound until a state of *kayf* is attained where a new openness about some subject is achieved, which is followed by a reflective period as the qat runs out and visitors make their way home. But as the Post Office clerks showed, it is chewed everywhere by everyone – even the police, while on duty.

One of the men who handed Charles the qat started talking.

'Where you come from?'

'Scotland,' Charles replied.

'In your country do you wear the *jambia*?' asked the man pointing to his dagger.

'No, but in Scotland we used to wear a *jambia* in our socks.'

A Somali standing next to us burst out laughing.

We left the Post Office and walked briskly up the road to visit the *mathaf* – The National Museum. This is housed in the former Royal Palace complex, built in 1932 by Imam Yahya. We walked through the entrance to be greeted by two larger than-life second century (AD) bronze figures. Both their style and inscriptions revealed Hellenistic influences. A Greek inscription on one of them, indicated that they had been made with the assistance of a sculptor named Phokas. The last time I saw them they were standing in an old shed-like building in 1983, just after their return from restoration in Germany.

Inside the museum, various floors are dedicated to pre-Islamic history, the Ottoman period and traditional arts and crafts, including building, weaving, indigo and silver work. Surprisingly little archaeology has taken place in Yemen, despite the fact that Yemen's history is crucial to the whole of Arabia. When I had visited the National Museum in 1983 it was a disorganised, cramped place, which reminded me of the Pitt Rivers Museum in Oxford. It had the same gentle ambience too. The museum had now been moved and modernised. During this first trip in the 1980s I had met the archaeologist Dr Selma Al-Radi. She had explained to me that every day somebody left some ancient artifact in the doorway of the museum.

'Yemenis are passionate about their history.'

Although the museum had originally been small, some four hundred locals came through the doors each day. Dr Al-Radi believed that there was nowhere else in the whole of Arabia, where this happened. In fact, a few days before I visited her she told me that a Bedouin had come into town by taxi, just to bring her an ancient sculpture he had found in the countryside. She was very excited by a group of mummies recently discovered that were believed to pre-date the Egyptian period.

Some ancient pre-Islamic Himyaritic carvings are the jewel of the museum. There are limited historical records about Arabia before Islam, but they include local rock engravings. But the most noteworthy of the artifacts date back to the Wendell Phillips expedition for the American Foundation for the Study of Man, in the early 1950s, particularly those of the *Awwam* Temple in Marib and the temple of Athtar in Timna. The excavation at Timna, the ruined capital of the Qataban Kingdom was to be the first of a complete temple in Southern Arabia. Robbers and looters had already taken their toll but important artifacts were found.

Wendell Phillips obtained permission to visit Imam Ahmed in Taiz in 1951 and negotiated permission to excavate in Marib. No large archaeological expedition had ever worked there. The area had the great romantic attraction of being linked to the Queen of Sheba. While Phillips raised funds, the team led by the biblical scholar Frank Albright spent about nine months there during 1951-2 working under a tremendous amount of pressure, suspicion and even hostility. The local tribes were not at all happy with the work at this remote site and demanded to keep all finds under their control.

At *Awwam*, the great temple of Marib – sometimes called *Mahram Bilqis* they dug deep. Dedicated to the moon god Almaqah the archeologist found a series of monolithic pillars, marking the entrance to the temple, which may have been used as a sanctuary. The finest sculpture of the ancient Arabs, a figurative bronze of a bearded Sabaean nobleman Ma'adi Karib, possibly sixth century B.C. and now in the National Museum, was found here. It is a striding figure dressed in a cloth kilt. A lionskin is draped over the back. It is an extraordinary work. But despite the great achievements of the dig, Phillips later wrote that one should not be romantic about such expeditions 'split lips, swollen tongues, frozen fingers, dysentery, fever, heartbreak, and monotony beyond compare are all major parts of the explorer's life.'

Aware that South Arabia was one of the last unknown and unexplored areas, he knew well that it was a place of uncertainty, difficulty and doubt. Marib was one of those parts of Yemen where the country was – and still is at times – run by the rifle, and blood feuds endure. Tribal genealogies go back into antiquity and the area looks back to the golden age of Yemen.

Phillips and his team were well aware of the importance of what they were doing. However, persistent harassment by local Yemenis finally compelled the archaeologists to leave, hastily crossing over the border to Bayhan in the British Protectorate, leaving behind their finds, many of which are now exhibited in the National Museum in Sana'a.

Research about the area showed that in the past, great camel trains (the camel was domesticated around 1,400 BC) had arrived here, carrying frankincense and myrrh, precious stones, and metals including gold and copper, even silk cloth, ivory and pearls; it was a crossroads of trade between Asia, Africa and Arabia. The camel caravans had established new trading kingdoms which took goods from the Indian Ocean to the Mediterranean, and created city trading posts on the way, including Marib, Najran, Mecca, Medina and Petra.

The wealth created by trade also supported the spiritual life of the region. Like the ancient Egyptians, the ancient Sabaeans believed in life after death, and the provision of goods in their tombs was a central tenet of this belief. The South Arabians built many temples to deities dedicated to the seasons, agriculture, and rains. Religious activity was paramount, and a large number of temples and shrines were erected during this period in history.

Religion was polytheistic involving worship around a triad of astral deities, the moon god Almaqah, sun goddess Shams and their son Athtar who was linked to Venus, the morning star. There were also gods of tribes and places, and irrigation deities. The many sun and moon temples that were built, a few of which have been excavated, hint at the extraordinary architectural skill and classical purity of form that existed at the time. Sabaean Art includes votive offerings and representations of bulls, horses, lions, vine-leaves, and camels, while architectural sculpture is notable for its friezes of ibex, bulls' head gargoyles, and animal spouts on sacrificial tables.

The most precious commodity carried by the camel caravans was incense, a simple aromatic resin from the bark of a tree. It was a prerequisite to please the gods as far away as Babylon, Jerusalem, and Egypt – where images are to be found of Kings offering homage to their gods by burning incense on the covers of ancient tombs. Ovid and Virgil describe how the Greek and Roman gods demanded its fragrance, and the Emperors desired it as a form of veneration.

The use of incense in worship has existed from the earliest of times throughout the Eastern and Western churches for festivals, processions, coronations, for purification in worship and to symbolise, by the rising smoke, the ascent of prayer before God. Even today in the Orthodox church the 'boat boy' hand carries the 'boat' laden with incense for the thurifer, who spoons it freely on to glowing coals, and spreads the fragrant odour, around the the congregation like a cloud.

Today Yemenis burn incense in their mosques during religious festivals, but also in the privacy of their homes to perfume their clothing and to sweeten the atmosphere; a host will often offer incense to his guests after a meal, an oblique signal to them that it is time to go. Moses was commanded by God to offer incense as a form of prayer and worship (Exodus 25:6) and in Luke 1:5-25 Zacharias was on duty burning incense when he was told by the angel Gabriel that his son John would be born and become filled with the Holy Spirit.

There was continuing strife between the ancient southern kingdoms of Arabia as they all depended on the trading links that hinged upon the burning of 'bakhur' or incense. The Arabic transitive verb *bakhara* means to evaporate, fumigate, to perfume with incense. *Bukhar* means vapour or steam. *Bakhira* is a steamship. All from the same root. The Latin *Incensum* means to 'set on fire' and Arab stokers were called 'firemen.' I could imagine the old Arab seamen watching a steamship offshore from Aden and visualising it as some great incense burner. Perhaps the burning of quality coal had a deeper psychological, cultural and spiritual importance than I had at first imagined.

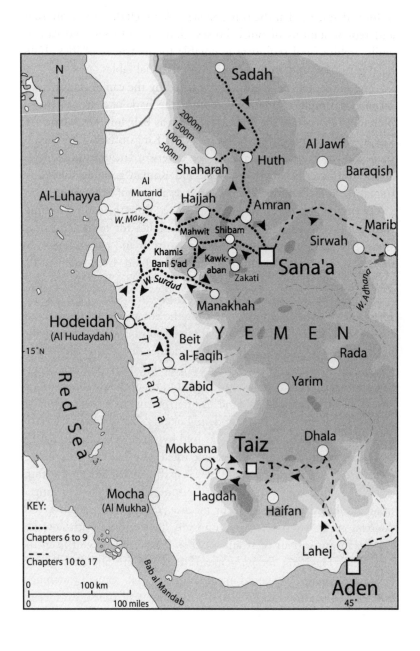

Beit Showta, Mahwit

Our Journey Is Ahead Of Us

'A wise man throws his shilling in the right place.'
(Yemeni proverb)

'Marco has written Sirwah on your itinerary,' said Khalid Awad, the Hadrami sales officer working for Universal Travel and Tourism. Running his eyes across the sheet of paper on his desk, he shook his head in disbelief.

'Marco brave man. You go to Sirwah?'

Sirwah and Marib had been the main centres of the first Southern Arabian trading empires which emerged around 1,000 BC. Sirwah is about 35 km west of Marib and some 120 km from Sana'a and was where Wendell Phillips had excavated.

Now it was reached by a tarmac road built in the early 1980s for the oilfields newly-discovered there. I knew the area could be problematic: vehicles were often hijacked or stolen. I had travelled to Marib on this same road in 1983, and passing the last army road blocks before winding down on to a wild and open plateau, you could sense the soldiers' apprehension as they waved us on. The tribes in the region did not recognise central government, and frequently fought each other – it was considered a sensitive area to travel in.

Khalid discussed the itinerary with us. We had spoken at length to Marco Livadiotti about what we wanted to do in Yemen. Our first and most important purpose was to photograph the country, and we had designed our itinerary around this. However, British and Welsh-Yemeni history was also important for our research and we had only five weeks to complete it all.

Khalid suggested we first visit some of the Yemeni highland

villages, many of which lay around 1,500 metres above sea level. Here we could photograph farmers in the terraced fields, a traditional way of life that had not altered for hundreds of years. Then would come the Tihama, the semi-desert area bordering the Red Sea. Travelling inland to Marib and Sirwah, we would cross the Ramlat as-Sabatayn desert accompanied by a Bedouin guide, to the Wadi Hadramaut to photograph the mud skyscrapers there. These towering structures were built with small mud bricks, in the same way as the Tower of Babel described in the book of Genesis. After this, we would return with Ahmed to the former British Colony of Aden via Mukalla and the coast road. This journey might well be a shock to Ahmed, who had grown up under British rule, and had not visited Aden since 1972. From there we would head back north.

'Are you happy with this?' asked Khalid.

'It seems fine to us,' replied Charles.

We agreed the final price for the vehicle and accommodation.

'We will organise a driver,' said Khalid and rushed out of the office.

Through the door came Naji Taher. He was about five foot six, stockily built, wearing a western style jacket over a brilliant white gown. The red and white checked *kaffiyah* wrapped around his head covered all but a few curls of black hair. He was heavily moustached. He looked us up and down before shaking hands, and then, seeing Marco, abruptly turned and went over to him. Judging from the tone of their discussion, there was a disagreement.

We returned to the Al-Ikhwa, packed, paid our bill, and headed for Bir Al-Azab, the garden city outside old Sana'a which the Ottomans built during their second occupation of Yemen in the latter half of the nineteenth century. Marco had arranged for us to stay in a house there which had once been the residence of the Turkish Governor, and had later been occupied by the American Embassy. It was a large mansion of interconnected rooms, plastered white, with traditional stained glass windows. Marco's dream was to restore it, employing local craftsmen, and to convert it into an hotel. Nobody else was staying while the building was under repair. The delightful walled garden included an orchard of pomegranate, orange and other fruit trees with flowering shrubs planted in between. Birds – bulbuls and the occasional pigeon – fluttered amongst the greenery. A few dogs sat lazily by the entrance. The tranquillity of the place was broken only by the muezzins calling the faithful to prayer.

We had been allocated a spacious white-washed room in one corner of the building. Two simple mattresses lay on the floor among some colourful locally-woven rugs. As is the case in many Yemeni houses, there was no furniture except a small table. Two wooden doors, carved with arabesques, led to an adjacent bathroom. A young Somali woman looked after our needs, providing breakfast each day. It was a haven of peace and comfort which we luckily had all to ourselves.

It took us some time to decide what we would take on our journey. I had packed a lot of books about Yemen, and had even paid excess baggage to bring them. *Arabia and the Isles* by Harold Ingrams, *The Southern Gates of Arabia* by Freya Stark, *Aden to the Hadramaut* by van der Meulen, *The Kingdom of Melchior* by The Master of Belhaven, and *Arabian Assignment* by David Smiley were a few sitting in my luggage. I decided that my enthusiasm for reading had taken precedence over the time we needed to research. Of course I realised now that I would not have time to read them or even have the energy to carry them with us across Yemen as we were travelling. I confidently left all but two (a 1960s British services handbook to Aden and a general guide) in a cupboard at Bir Al-Azab.

With our camera bags safely at our feet, we waited for sunrise and then packed everything into the Toyota Landcruiser. Naji seemed in a good mood, and was singing to himself. We had arranged to meet Ahmed outside the Ministry of Tourism. He was waiting for us on the kerb, and jumped into the vehicle with the enthusiasm of a man temporarily liberated from the cares of office life.

'Our journey is ahead of us,' he observed sententiously. He was clutching a guide book, or, rather, a commentary by the tenth-century Yemeni geographer and historian, Al-Hamdani. Recent guides to Yemen were few and far between, so Ahmed had chosen a classic.

'Here is the documentation the Ministry has given us,' said Ahmed, handing us a sheet of Arabic typescript. This roughly translated as:

Yemeni Republic, Ministry of Tourism,
Date: 5-7-1992, No 309

To whom it may concern,
Mr Charles Aithie and his wife Patricia Aithie are preparing to publish
a documentary & informative book in the field of tourism and they
are planning to make a documentary & touristic film on the same
subject. They will go on a discovery tour to all touristic sites in the
country. We beg of you to be kind enough to offer all possible help to
them. Brother Ahmed Abdul Halim, will accompany them.

Accept our intense salutations.
Abdul Majeed Wahdin
Head of the Tourism Board

Copy with salutations to brother, head of human resources.

Naji started up the car, drove ahead for a hundred yards and
stopped.

'What's the problem?' I asked.

Ahmed turned and looked at us.

'Naji says he needs to eat meat.'

'We have travelled only one hundred yards and the driver needs to
eat meat?' asked Charles.

'Yes. He says he can't move any further without eating. That he
needs to eat meat like the vehicle needs petrol to function.'

Naji parked the Landcruiser up on the pavement with the authority of someone who had shares in the restaurant he had stopped
outside.

Inside, the room was crammed with laminated tables with men
eating amidst a cacophony of sound and laughter and the clatter of
metal plates. They ate as if it was the last food they would ever see and
with such speed it gave a new meaning to the phrase 'fast food'. We
found a place to sit down. Ahmed wiped the table top with some
tissue. Naji rushed towards the kitchens.

'He's checking the meat.' said Ahmed. 'He will only eat the best he
says, and needs to check the meat before it is cooked.'

'What meat is it?' I asked Naji on his return.

'Lamb. You only eat chicken and lamb. Eating beef is like eating a car!' replied Naji. 'A cow is the same size!'

Having fed sumptuously we headed for the road out of Sana'a with raised spirits. Our main aim was to reach the mountain village of Kawkaban by nightfall. Leaving the city we passed fields scattered with totem-like piles of stones, a Yemeni version of scarecrows. An old British truck which appeared to be abandoned on a plot of land had instead been recycled to pump water for irrigation. The landscape was dusty and volcanic, not the rich verdant greens we had expected but an unremitting beige. Perched on every outcrop of rock stood fortifications which doubled as homes. A large lorry in front of us was driving on the wrong side of the road causing us to swerve and nearly landing us in the rubble by the roadside.

'You are like Britanni, Britanni', Naji shouted at the offending driver. He was alluding to the British practice of driving on the left which continued in Aden long after independence.

'Maybe they should change the side they drive on,' said Charles, clinging to his seat in the back.

'You are right!', said Naji, 'Just like Aden!'

'Don't worry,' said Ahmed quietly. 'Naji's name means 'rescued from danger'.

The Arabs have a saying that it is not good for the soul to travel faster than the trot of a camel, but it looks like Naji is going to break all the rules.

Naji grumbled something in Arabic.

'He says he started driving when he was ten, so he knows what he's doing.'

Naji turned his head to Ahmed. He looked unimpressed, and then spoke rapidly, as he put his foot down on the accelerator and we disappeared in a cloud of dust.

Then came the story of Naji's life.

'He says he started driving when he was ten while living in Saudi Arabia. His father was a guard in a Royal household. Naji would drive for hunting parties in the desert.'

Naji lifted himself off his seat as if to suggest he was too small at the time to sit down and instead drove standing up.

'He then worked as a tanker driver, then moved to taxis,'

Naji was laughing, looking at Ahmed he said 'Now tourists!'.

'He's been driving tourists for over seventeen years, longer than probably just about anyone in Yemen. He knows Europeans well,' said Ahmed.

This was true, as we were later to find out. 'Why don't you have this?' said Naji pointing to his moustache and looking at Charles, in his mirror.

'The bigger the moustache the more Naji likes you,' laughed Ahmed who bore a neat grey one.

'Like Saddam and Stalin, for example?' said Charles with an impish grin.

We stopped at the villages of Thula and Hababa to photograph their superb stone architecture honeycombed with round alabaster windows. Then we crossed the plain of Al-Munakab, once densely wooded but now treeless and terraced for cultivation. Seasonal crops here include barley, wheat, lentils, beans and fenugreek. At harvest time whole families are to be seen cutting the crop, bringing it in from the fields or threshing grain. In the absence of their menfolk working abroad, women have become actively involved in farming, although ploughing and digging are still usually left to men.

'Look', said Naji, pointing towards the sky, 'we go there'.

'Where?', I asked.

'Up there, Kawkaban', said Ahmed. 'The village on the top, can't you see?'

'You mean we are going up there?', I said as my eye focused on a cluster of houses clinging to the edge of the high mountain escarpment ahead of us. I could see why Yemen was sometimes called the 'Roof of Arabia'.

We started up a rough, twisting track which was not then for the faint-hearted but has since been tarmacked and is now a relatively swift and comfortable ride. Our tyres kicked up clouds of dust as they dug into the gravel. We passed an old graveyard with headstones of finely cut basalt.

'In Yemen when people die', remarked Ahmed, 'we wrap them in a simple cloth with perfume and scented leaves – no jewellery; you leave the way you were born.'

It made me think of the multitudinous slate gravestones in Welsh cemeteries. Someone once wrote '...to live in Wales is to know that the dead still outnumber the living', evoking the melancholy and sombre sense of history which is so much part of the Welsh soul. As we climbed, the views across the broad swathe of green terraced fields towards the mountain ridge above Thula were breathtaking. We stopped a short distance below Kawkaban to admire its walls and tower houses bathed in the golden light of the late afternoon sun. A lone shepherd was herding his flock towards the town's fortified gateway, past a large cistern brimming with rainwater. Mirrored on its calm surface, the sheep seemed to double in number.

Kawkaban was built to serve as a refuge for the inhabitants of Shibam which lies at the foot of the escarpment and is linked to Kawkaban by a steep paved footpath which takes about an hour to climb. It must have been one of Yemen's most impregnable and strategically important strongholds, and was often under siege, notably by the Ayyubid commander Tughtakin (brother of the better known Saladin) who ruled Yemen from 1173 to 1228; and later, during the second half of the sixteenth century, by the Ottoman commander Sinan Pasha.

In 1896 the Turks again besieged and occupied Kawkaban, and during the civil war of 1962-67 the town was heavily bombed by the Egyptians. Today much of Kawkaban, including many of its fine tower houses, lie in ruins, and it has rather a desolate atmosphere.

We headed through the town towards the local hotel, a traditional stone-built residence with a strikingly decorative façade, and characteristic tympanum inside. We climbed up the great staircase that is the centre of every large Yemeni house.

'Why, when people take so much trouble to walk up great mountain-sides to get to their houses, do they have to add to their troubles by building houses that make you continue even further upwards. To cap it all they put the main sitting room on the top floor – it's just beyond me,' said Charles.

'When you see the room with the view you will understand the reason why,' responded Ahmed.

That night we had lamb and *shafout* – crepes immersed in yoghurt or buttermilk with chillis, garlic and coriander. After dinner I sat outside for a while, watching the pale sky vanishing under a pall of dark cloud as the sun set, until a sharp chill in the air brought me inside to seek the relative warmth of our candle-lit room.

I had hoped that next morning would be clear and sunny, but all I could see from our window was heavy mist. We spent more than an hour outside waiting for the mist, actually cloud, to lift so that we could start taking photographs. Visibility was so poor that we could easily have plunged over a precipice if we had not taken great care. As the morning warmed up the cloud retreated and blew across the flat windy plain on which we stood. It felt strange to be at such altitude. I tried to find a point of focus on the vast landscape below. The view was magnificent, miles of undulating rock outcrops with soft green shrubbery and plants. We took our pictures and returned for breakfast. Scrambled eggs, local bread and sweet tea. Ahmed joined us, then Naji. We were going to Zakati today.

'Zakati has meat,' exclaimed Naji.

Zakati takes its name from *zakat*, the annual religious tax paid by Muslims. It is some thirty kilometres from Kawkaban: no road, only a track through grassland reminiscent of the Mongolian steppe, where flocks of black sheep grazed; and on through fields of grain, lentils and beans. We saw an agamid lizard running across the ground on its hind legs, a very rare sight. It is a species which, like chameleons, is renowned for changing colour, but an agamid alters colour rather more dramatically, in response to mood-swings and instinct.

We heard a flute being played, and according to Ahmed this was an accomplishment which pastoralists were born to. Proverbs, he added, were also a feature of popular Yemeni culture.

'We speak in proverbs – sayings fill every sentence', he said.

'We have a saying in Britain which goes: 'a bird in hand is worth two in the bush'. 'Do you have anything like this?', I asked.

'Yes, in Yemen we say: 'a bird in hand is worth ten in the tree".

There is a saying in highland Yemen that a man should be able to do three things – fire a gun, dance and compose poetry. As one might expect in a primarily rural society, Yemeni poems and songs are full of themes about farming and the land; but a youth's first compositions are usually on the subject of love, or to glorify his tribe or to satirise an enemy. The first line in many Yemeni poems should invoke God's name, just like so many hymns.

In their feeling for poetry Yemenis are not unlike the Welsh. The earliest poem in the Welsh/Brythonic language (and the earliest poem written in Scotland) is the *Gododdin*, a Welsh word for the Votadini tribe who lived in the Edinburgh region during and after the Roman occupation. The long poem comments on the ill-fated but heroic expedition of the Celtic tribe to Catraeth (Catterick, in north Yorkshire) to fight against the invading Saxons and is attributed to the poet Aneirin. Poets in Wales are held in the highest esteem, and all through Britain poets have kept us aware of who we are and why we exist. It has been said that the more a society separates from its roots and traditions, the more it loses its soul, and its art and poetry deteriorate. Certainly for the Arabs their history lies within their verse, as there is no Pre-Islamic poetry written down. It has been preserved by oral tradition alone. Ahmed, who listened to the BBC World Service at night, surprised us the following morning with the news that he had heard a programme about poets and musicians from the Eisteddfod.

Reaching Zakati, we stopped on the edge of the village to a warm welcome from a local family who were quick to offer us refreshment. Loaves of unleavened bread were brought to us, along with sweet herbal tea.

'Chi? Chi?' They asked cheerfully.

'Yes, tea would be lovely,' I replied and we sat down on a small dry-stone wall.

'It has been raining,' said Ahmed. 'They have been blessed again.'

The old man pointed towards a rock face.

'He wants to know if you would like to see the old village and the mosque?' said Ahmed. 'But he said we must be careful, it has been raining and the stones may make you slip.'

We finished our tea and were led to a narrow street running through a cleft in the rockside. Nearby stood a large medieval granary, constructed from hewn blocks of stone set one upon another with amazing precision. We passed a group of girls wrapped up from head to foot – like butterflies in a chrysalis.

'I'm told the women here are very beautiful,' said Ahmed. 'Have you heard about the man who went to look for a wife for his son? When he saw the girl, he married her himself! Divorce is very common; forty to forty five percent of people in Yemen divorce. Shariah law allows divorce but it is the worst possible scenario. However it is not legal if the woman is pregnant or until forty days after the birth.'

'What about children?' I asked.

'Children should stay with their mother, if possible up until seven years of age; but if the women marries and the husband does not like the new husband he can take the children back. He is allowed to take children over seven years, and sometimes a judge can ask the children where they want to go before they go anywhere.'

We continued up the narrow street until it met a cliff-face towering above us. We were close to a precipice which plunged down to the terraced landscape below. The drop was awe-inspiring, but a youth stood nonchalantly on the very edge, smoking a cigarette. We made our way tentatively round the cliff-side towards a group of single and double storey stone houses. They were small and neat as in a Welsh valley street, yet seemed infinitely older.

Nestled below the cliff face was a tiny mosque and beside it a cistern for ablutions. The man and a few boys who had followed us suggested we might like to go inside the mosque. But through the doorway we could see someone praying inside. We stayed outside until he finished and Charles, taking off his shoes, entered quietly. Seeing the shoes left outside, the old man repeatedly said in Arabic, 'What a good man, what a good man, he must be from a good family.' The mosque was probably seven hundred years old, and the local people seemed very proud of it. A large rich red carpet lay on the floor, looking as if it had been plucked from the air. That was the sort of place Zakati was, a place where unusual things could happen. The people were good hospitable people and we felt privileged to have met them.

We decided to attempt the drive to the mountainous terraced region of Al Mahwit via At-Tawila. The area is known as one of the most beautiful in Yemen, but the roads at times are precipitous and

The old Mosque at Zakati

twist and turn suddenly and dangerously. The first village we came to
was Al Ahjour. Above us on a rock was a ruined *nobah* – a watch
tower, sometimes also used for grain storage. It reminded me of one
of the ancient brochs of Scotland. Such towers are scattered throughout Yemen, and are often of great antiquity. It is not unusual to see a
person perched inside guarding a field of qat, sorghum or vines.

We dropped down into the valley below, passing patches of green
cultivation among huge boulders, some the size of a large house, many
precariously balanced. In the distance a waterfall tumbled over a cliff.
There were orchards of fruit trees and terraced fields of qat. Women
and children were tilling between rows of neatly planted crops. Soon
we could see the distinctive rocky outcrop of Tawila among slopes
wooded with acacia trees and half veiled in mountain mist.

Above every village perched a fort or watchtower but I could see
no minarets and asked Ahmed why.

'Because there is no need to call anyone to prayer. They are all
small communities and everyone knows each other.'

'What about travellers?', I asked.

'When you are travelling you do not have to pray the full five times a day. The people of this area are known to be very peaceful, more like Tihama people than mountain people'.

Eventually we turned down a track which wound along a terraced mountainside towards Mahwit. Many of the terraces had been neglected, as men left the fields to work abroad, and had begun to crumble.

At Mahwit we knocked at the door of a house to ask if we could have a room for the night. The woman living there agreed and welcomed us in. We were taken to the upper room, the *mafraj*. It was about thirty feet long with white stucco work and stained glass windows. Rugs were thrown across the floor and stiff cushions to sit on lay around the edge of the room. We settled down and I looked out through a window. In the street, I could see pillows being brought into the house in a wheel barrow.

'I go to car,' said Naji.

'Why?'

'Maybe somebody take car – where do I get a car from here?'

Charles suggested he took out the distributor. We all started joking about how we could dismantle the car and put it back together again in the morning.

Ahmed went out to get water, bread and yoghurt. When he returned the woman who ran the house came through the door, in great black and yellow striped pantaloons and brought us some Nescafé. She started joking and laughing with Ahmed.

'She said the people next door have eight sets of twins.'

'Eight sets?'

'Yes eight.'

'My next-door neighbour in Wales had ten children,' I said. Ahmed translated.

'Was she in the newspaper?' came back in Arabic, surprised that a western family would have so many.

'No.'

'Then she is Yemeni! God should give us only two or three children.'

Yemen has one of the highest population growths in the world, at around 3.4% a year. In rural Yemen women have an average of eight children. It is believed the number of Yemenis could double in the next twenty years, a sobering thought for the country despite the discovery of oil and gas.

The door of our room had been left ajar. Outside we could see a long chain of men as they entered a nearby *mafraj*, carrying water-pipes – *mada'ah*, and plastic bags full of qat. It was not long before smoke pervaded our room. Sounds of hilarity from our neighbours continued late into the night. We stretched out on the cushions and finally fell asleep.

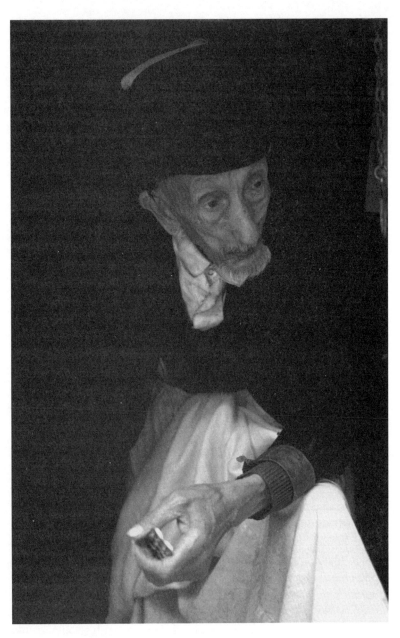

Old man in Al Hajjarah

Coffee and Jinns

'Two people meet on the street and one says
'How is the market today?'
'Why do you ask me about the market?' came
the reply. 'You are going there yourself!'

'In 15 minutes we get hot weather,' said Naji looking at us through his rear-view mirror, and wiping his brow.

He wasn't joking, we descended quickly from the cool mountain ranges down into a heat reminiscent of a blast furnace. We were heading towards the flat Tihama coastal plain, with a humid and enervating climate and none of the drama of the highlands. Geologically it is an extension of the Rift Valley system of East Africa.

Naji turned on the air-conditioner.

'I told you Yemen is a country that has four seasons at one time,' joked Ahmed as we all perspired. Although Yemen is perhaps the most verdant area of the Arabian Peninsula, with the highest rainfall, it has the contrast of ice in some winter months in the mountains and extreme heat and deserts. The coastal plain we now entered was harsh, hot and humid – hardly tolerable even in winter, or when the many *wadis* are in spate.

Small compact villages of conical thatched huts replaced the tall stone houses, earthen dykes, stone terraces, and fields of cotton, millet, maize and tobacco began to appear. Leaner and darker figures rode on camels and donkeys. It was a reminder of how close we were to Africa, and how long Yemen has been trading with that continent.

We drove through Wadi Hofash, around us were flowering bottle trees, *Adenium obesum*. These extraordinary trees with swollen trunks are found all over the dry mountain slopes of the Tihama foothills.

Yemen was once completely covered in woodland but, over millennia, has been cleared for agriculture, grazing and the endless quest for firewood and timber. But there are still succulents, scrub and grasses, and many plants found in East Africa abound here too. The central highlands are now completely deforested, as a consequence of an ever expanding population. Not far from where we were travelling lay Jebel Bura, which rises to 2271 metres, and is one of the last vestiges of extensive subtropical forest in the Arabian Peninsula: It lies at a latitude of 15° north and is difficult to reach so the sparse local population has exerted less pressure on the forest's resources. As a result it still supports a vast variety of migratory birds and butterflies. Large groups of baboons roam the forest's floor, as well as hyenas, and until recently, leopards.

We entered rock strewn Wadi Surdud. Streams of water gushed across our path, shady trees bent over us, blocking the view to the jungle-like slopes around us. Bright yellow Ruppell's weaverbirds flitted about, and tended their nests in the tall reed beds. A boy saluted us from his donkey, people walked by carrying bundles of firewood while a young man selling qat wrapped in banana leaves vied for our attention. A woman in a nearby field tended a cow. Here in Wadi Surdud local women compose poems, which they recite or sing to their cows, hoping that their words will increase milk production. It seemed the right place to celebrate life, in this fertile region with its aromatic flowers and abundant fruit.

Utterly exhausted by the constant bumping on the suspension and the increasing heat, we decided to stop near a corrugated iron shack where hot food was sold. The kitchen was cluttered with steaming metal pots with today's offering precariously balanced on a makeshift stove. Eating was a serious business again. We ate *helba* – a lamb dish with garlic, coriander, cumin and fenugreek, served in a black earthenware vessel – it is famous in Yemen for settling the stomach before chewing qat. We ate in silence. Naji emptied the base of the bowl with huge chunks of bread. The midday heat did not suit our two Yemeni travelling companions. Nor did it suit a man walking nearby who shouted in Arabic at the restaurant owners.

'What do you live in a place like this for?'

We paid for the meal, it was expensive but then the Landcruiser had miraculously filled with qat by the time we had left. The temperature in the back of the vehicle was unbearable. Naji was visibly irritated by the heat. Ahmed, who had grown up with the intense heat of Aden, was more passive and thoughtful. We found a smooth tarmacked road again and things improved.

The road between Sana'a and Hodeidah is 246 kilometres long and one of many that the Chinese helped to build. We had seen the Chinese cemetery outside Sana'a, Chinese characters etched on to the sides of gravestones commemorating the people who died far from home cutting roads through the precipitous mountains of Yemen. We were winding our way down to the sea and up again, heading for Manakhah for our evening stop. At 2,200 metres above sea level, the town sits on a narrow ridge high up in the Haraz mountains. The Ottomans established a garrison here because it was an important market town and vital communications link between Sana'a and Hodeidah. It was also an important gathering point for the valuable coffee traded through the coastal port of Mocha. Like most rural markets in Yemen, Manakhah was full of imported goods – fizzy drinks, music cassettes, biscuits wrapped in plastic stacked next to drawers of spices, coffee husks and locally carved implements. Here, like everywhere else in the region, money is spent on qat.

The *funduq* (hotel) in Manakhah was a four storey stone house, built before anyone in the village could remember. There were few facilities except the luxury of a western style toilet and a small wash basin from which freezing cold water flowed in abundance. Charles was unshaven and I was beginning to realise why perfume was so prized in this country. I was longing for a hot bath. Proverbs 27:9 was right, 'Perfume and incense bring joy to the heart.' But the owners were kind and could not do enough to make us happy.

That night the windows rattled and outside the trees creaked in a raging wind. We were told that the area was renowned for *jinn* – (according to Muslim belief spirits with supernatural powers over humans) that live in the trees. If the wind continued without abating the *jinn* would come inside. I woke up in the night feeling as if someone was sitting on my chest; I could hardly breathe. I was later to learn that this is a well-recognised form of sleep paralysis, which can affect you if you suddenly awake from deep REM sleep.

Charles and I rose at 5.45am. It was only just light. We put our camera bags over our shoulders and hoping to give Ahmed and Naji a rest we hiked up the mountain road towards Al Hajjarah, a village perched on the next ridge. The distant view of Al Hajjarah was spectacular. Like Kawkaban it can be seen for miles, crowning the hilltop. Its great fortress structure seems to be a natural continuation of the steep cliff below. It is a masterpiece of Yemeni vernacular architecture, forming an uninterrupted rampart, built without mortar, and sensational and awe-inspiring in scale. Clouds hung in the valleys and the village appeared like an island in a sea of mist.

We found ourselves amongst a sprawl of agricultural terraces that resembled a mammoth Roman amphitheatre. Sometime later one of Yemen's premier artists, Fuad al Futaih, told me that a friend of his went into a remote village in this region and found all the local people in masks enacting some ancient pagan or animist ritual, perhaps intended to ensure a good harvest. In Medieval Wales farmers and pilgrims used to collect water from Holy Springs in small clay vessels or scallop shaped ampullae and bury them in the fields for the same purpose.

Above, a man was calling to his friend below down in the valley, the echoes of their voices reverberated off the surrounding hills. A lone figure chipped away at a nearside rock face with a simple flat ended tool, producing superbly crafted blocks. Later that morning we saw these blocks loaded into a pick-up truck and taken back to the village masons.

About three quarters of the way up the road, I felt a twinge in my ankle. It began to hurt badly, so we stopped and rested for a while, absorbing the landscape before us.

Charles set up his tripod and Hasselblad and took out a wide angle lens. The image through the viewfinder was staggering. The forbidding sky, with patches of bright ultramarine, gave colour to the great medieval structures. After a while I took some black and white photographs on my Nikon using an 80-200mm lens, trying to get closer to the buildings. I never like my pictures to look too wide, too distant, but I have been judged in the past for being too close, and using a 35mm camera is sometimes frowned on. Charles' camera looked impressive, but it was too slow and deliberate for me. I like my camera to be as discreet as possible. Only then do the interesting photographs arise. I wanted to highlight the striking abstract white gypsum decoration splashed across the house facades. The photograph unlike the landscape, or portrait it has captured, never changes.

Entering Al Hajjarah by way of a series of steep steps and through a small gateway, we came to a small shop where an elderly man sat hunched. He had the longest, palest face I have ever seen and cheeks sunken beneath a black woollen turban. His coat was black too. He looked so old and was possibly of Turkish descent. Yemen is sometimes called the 'Graveyard of the Turks' with reference to the Ottoman occupation which ended in 1918. Nearby Manakhah had been an important garrison town where remnants of Turkish dress and even vocabulary still linger. I thought of Abdul Wali, the stoker in Cardiff speaking about his catapults. I tried unobtrusively to take photographs.

'Ah, please, please,' he said, beckoning us.

'Yes?' asked Charles.

The old man pointed to his knees. He looked at us and pointed again.

'Ah, Ah.'

'He needs aspirin,' came a softly spoken voice from our right. 'He often asks visitors. I am his son. Can you help?'

Our medicine was back at the *funduq* so Charles promised to bring him some the next day. In fact we delivered it later that evening.

When we returned to the shop the man's son, who looked about seventy years old himself, was crushing cumin seeds in a mortar and pestle. He told us that his father had gone to the mosque to pray. But said 'You are very kind, even if it had been your own father, tomorrow would have done!'

We left the village on a road well maintained for sheep and donkeys, but narrow. I mentioned to Naji about the wind the previous night, and the *jinn*.

'You must be careful,' he said startled. '*jinn* are everywhere.' He began to relate a story.

Some years previously when he was driving for a Japanese television crew they went to film in Shabwa, the foremost ancient pre-Islamic site in Yemen, on the edge of the desert. They had had a busy day filming and, at the end of the day, camped nearby. It was late when Naji saw it. 'Maybe eleven o'clock. We were sitting talking. Voices and music came from the old city and we saw a pink and orange light with people moving amongst the ruins. I believe it was *jinn*,' he said nervously.

Later Naji insisted I wore a bracelet of woven goats hair made by his grandfather, for protection against the evil eye.

After lunch we headed for Al Hotaib, an Ismaili shrine up a track behind Manakhah where pilgrims congregate from as far afield as India. The road was rough, and we soon stopped, sat on a rock and admired one of the best views in Yemen. We were up high, and mountain after mountain rolled out before us like waves. On each rocky outcrop stood a fortified village surrounded by rows of coffee bushes, neatly planted on sunbathed terraces and watered by the regular monsoon winds blowing from India. It was from remote villages like these that coffee (now the world's second most traded commodity) spread across the world in the seventeenth century, through Yemen's coastal port of Mocha, where the British and Dutch had established factories in 1618. Sufi mystics were, according to legend, the first to drink it as it promotes alertness during their devotional practices, and it spread with them through the mosques to Egypt, Syria and Istanbul. But it was the Ottoman Turks who introduced it into Europe, where it was enthusiastically received after their defeat at the gates of Vienna in 1683. The Ottomans knew full well the economic value of the crops in this region and protected it militarily. Of course now everyone has heard of 'Turkish coffee', but like 'English tea' it was not grown in Turkey but rather traded by them.

The coffee trade reached its peak around 1730 as tremendous rivalry existed between the Dutch, British and French who all vied for control. The trade made the region wealthy until seedlings were smuggled out to Africa, South America, and the Dutch East Indies. It is a remarkable fact that practically all the coffee in the world today has come from this original Yemeni root-stock. Coffee houses sprang up all over Europe and in the 1680s Edward Lloyd opened a coffee house near the London Docklands. It was a favourite place for captains, merchants and other men working on the ships moored nearby. Moving to Lombard Street, Lloyd published *Lloyds List*, (London's oldest daily newspaper) in 1696, which gave all kinds of information about shipping. The coffee house became a place where people swapped maritime information; ships' auctions took place and eventually it witnessed the birth of the world's most famous insurance company. Wealthy men shared risk by signing a policy agreeing to cover an amount, and their names which were positioned one beneath another, became known as 'underwriters'. Interestingly it was in 1871, two years after the opening of the Suez canal and the expansion of the shipping routes, that the Lloyd's Act was passed by Parliament, setting a legal framework for its activities. It is no coincidence that the London Stock Exchange was also started in a coffee house.

Cardiff has one of the biggest importers of coffee in Britain, The Costa Rica Coffee Co., founded by a Cardiff sea captain and his brother in 1924. It was originally situated at Great Western Approach, right on the canal which stretched down to the docks, but is now based in the Pontcanna area of the city. Martin Borg, the new owner, is the son of a Maltese sailor who settled in Cardiff. He showed me an old stock book listing the names of clients supplied by the company. Apart from cafes such as the Greek Sailors Club, Dutch Cafe, Empire Cafe, British Council, RAF St Athans, The Officers Mess, Brecon, and even a cafe called Mecca in Porthcawl, the company supplied nearly every Italian cafe in the Welsh valleys. Italian cafes spread throughout the mining villages of south Wales and became one of the favourite places for miners families to enjoy time off. It surprised me to learn that while these miners were digging up coal to send out to Aden, they were consuming in vast quantities of a drink that had originated in Yemen. The Costa Rica Coffee Co. stock book in the 1940s lists clients including: Forte, Barry; Servini, Blackwood; Bracchi, Tonypandy; Sidoli, Merthyr; Conte, Caermarthen; Carpanneri, Porth; Rossi, Ebbw Vale; Gazzi, Maesteg; Maruzzi, Caerphilly; Gucci, Hirwaen; as well as cafes in Bute Street.

* * *

'What do you think of the architecture then?' asked Ahmed sweeping his hand across the landscape.

'It is unbelievable. Unlike anything I have seen.' I said.

I thought of the old proverb 'An Arab is a man who will pull down a whole temple to have a stone to sit on.'

'We Yemenis have a joke.' said Ahmed. 'When the American astronauts arrived on the moon they were met by three Yemenis. They asked them 'Where are you from?'

'From Yemen' came the reply.

'Why are you here?' they asked the first.

'To find a new gun' came the reply.

They looked at the second. 'Why are you here?'

'To find better qat' he said. Then to the third they asked the same question.

'I am here to build something of course!'

'There you see' said Ahmed. 'the three aspects of our society! They say in Yemen that one good house well built is better than a destroyed village, surely this region proves that'.

Charles wandered off down the road carrying his Hasselblad and tripod over his shoulder. Ahmed, Naji and I returned to the four wheel drive. We were exchanging the kind of thoughts that arrive in such elevated places when Ahmed suddenly asked 'Why is Charles taking so long?'

Naji shrugged his shoulders and then looked in his wing mirror. Like a sprinter out of starting blocks, he opened the door and ran.

'Where the hell has he gone now?' shouted Ahmed.

We looked behind us and in the distance we could see Naji bending, gesturing at the cliff edge and reaching out.

'Something has happened.' I said, peering after him. I turned back and Ahmed had disappeared too. I caught them up just in time to see Charles upside down, his feet in the air, his head pointing down the hill towards a coffee plantation and his Hasselblad being handed over to Naji with one hand, whilst clinging to a small shrub with the other.

Naji was pleased with himself for saving the camera and Charles was now free to swivel on the loose stones. With years of running experience he came up the side of the hill like a goat. Ahmed once again reminded us to be careful where we stood after the rains.

Back at the *funduq* my ankle was getting worse. I had never had a problem with it before but that night I was in terrible pain. The woman running the *funduq* insisted that I put it in very hot water for an hour, which I did. Then it was covered in oil, with plenty of salt, and was bound very tightly. It was like tenderising meat.

'Salt goes into the muscle at that temperature,' said Ahmed. By next morning, my ankle was healed.

That night we ate lamb and Bint As Sahan (Daughter of the Plate), a pastry topped with lashings of local honey, cooked in a clay oven. You never dine frugally in Yemen. We sat and listened to a local musician play the 'ud or lute, an instrument much favoured by Yemenis. Under Imam Yayha and Imam Ahmed music had been suppressed, but today musicians and singers enjoy cult status throughout the country and are popular in the Gulf. In the room sat another driver, who was also staying in the *funduq*. He was the spitting image of Peter Sellers, his speech was very deliberate and resembled a 1950s BBC broadcaster. He sat in the corner with his back against the wall, as still as a Buddha.

'What do you think of Hodeidah and Beit al-Faqih? I understand it is one of the best markets in the world, and certainly the best in the Arabian Peninsula. We are heading there tomorrow.' I asked hoping to begin a conversation.

He raised his eyebrows, and looked thoughtfully at us. I noticed everyone in the room listened very carefully to everything he said.

'Two people meet on the street and one says 'How is the market today?' 'Why do you ask me about the market.' came the reply. 'You are going there yourself!'

I turned to the driver once again, believing there was more to this man with the impeccable English accent. I asked about local proverbs, holding my notebook in my hand.

'A good sleep is better than a camel full of gold,' he said smiling, as Naji, who slept easily and was already reclining like a Roman, raised his eyebrows in disbelief.

'Before you buy a house, find out who your neighbours are,' was received with nods from all round the room. He continued. 'I taught my friend to shoot, he shot me.' Everyone laughed uncontrollably.

The Tihama

Dwelling Place of the Ottomans

'Better a craft than wealth.' (Welsh saying)

We left Manakhah early next morning in high spirits. The clouds hovered over the mountain ridges doing their best to keep the intense morning sun, which gave a shimmering silver cast to the snake-like road before us, at bay. Our aim was to get to the port of Hodeidah via Khamis Bani Sa'd, through which we had fleetingly passed the day before. Today, Thursday, was the weekly market day. Weekly markets are held throughout Yemen. Usually named after the village or day of the week, they are places of no settled community where people gather in a neutral zone or 'hijrah' set aside from tribal conflict.

By the time we arrived at Khamis Bani Sa'd, there were hundreds of men around us, all clad in white cotton with a *futa* (kilt-like skirt) and straw hats, walking through the market. All kinds of small temporary structures had been set up to make trading spaces and offer a little shade. Canopies of reeds and hessian sackcloth were draped across rows of disjointed wooden frames. Other people had set up on the *wadi*'s edge, with local pottery or a few woven baskets by their sides. Many had produce simply strewn across the ground.

Women walked and traded freely. After the *sharshafs* (black shrouds) worn by women in the highlands, it was a relief to me to see them unveiled, emerging from the shade in colourful cotton dresses, daringly revealing the upper part of their bosoms. Some dresses were black, but they were embroidered with thick cotton rope-like patterns that would have made any mariner proud and with a few swirling designs imitated the oldest symbol in the world – the sun.

Men sold *halwah* (Turkish Delight) and sweets made of peanuts and honey. Dates, oranges, coconuts, papayas and lemons, brought in from local groves, were piled on to tables. Nearby, trucks, camels and donkeys laden with produce, struggled across Wadi Surdud through a metre or so of water. The local market in the Tihama is a lifeline for many.

The sweltering heat beat down directly on our heads. My temples were pounding. Life in the Tihama is harsh. The mean temperature can reach up to 50°C (122°F). And if that wasn't enough of a curse, humidity can reach almost 100%. In early spring and late summer, the rains arrive and rejuvenate the forests. Mangrove swamps run the length of the narrow strip of coastline, as far north as Saudi Arabia.

The people, too are very different to the highland Arabs. They still use dialects, words and accents with African elements brought by traders, and slaves over the centuries. The Red Sea is not much more than 250 miles wide at any point and small trading craft can cross it. In these communities the veneration of local saints and the pre-Islamic healing practises confirm a different life to the stricter observance of Islamic doctrines further inland. The people of Tihama like the people of the southern mountains, have been predominantly Shafi'i (Sunni) and tolerate these practices.

In the early 800s AD the capital of Yemen came to Zabid in the Tihama and continued there into the early medieval period. Zabid became a great university town, a magnet for culture with distinct characteristics, and craftsmanship of weaving and indigo dyeing. The region produced the Rasulids, a ruling dynasty which built some of the finest architecture still existing in Yemen and reflecting a knowl-edge of the outside Arab world. By the late Medieval period political power had moved elsewhere, but as a trading centre it never lost its importance. Many nations have traded along the Red Sea and many Tihamans were mediators between foreign powers and the high-landers. Due to this, and the fact that it sits on the edge of a major sea thoroughfare, the Tihama more than any other part of Yemen has seen waves of invasions and occupations. Because the land is flat it is easy to control and often fell under the occupation of the rulers of Asir or Abu Arish to the north. The Ottomans built many fortresses here, while the highland north at times remained in the hands of the Imams who were often rejected by the local Tihaman sheikhs, who as non-

Zaidis, adopted the Sunni branch of Islam. Marauding Portuguese, and the Mamluks from Egypt, also tried their hand at taking parts of the Tihama. The importance of its coastal ports only diminished once the British took Aden in 1839.

The highlanders have often viewed the Tihaman people as a different race. The fact that the north frequently dominated the area bred a marked distrust between the two regions, although the highlanders praise Tihamans for their honesty.

We continued on our journey past Bajil and on to flat sandy plains with mud huts, and mounds of harvested sorghum stalks destined for animal fodder. All around us the horizons were empty and made even flatter by the stormy grey of the sky. Then the landscape changed, bright fields of cotton, maize, sorghum, bananas and melons added texture. We passed dilapidated Russian cement works. Huge modern advertising hoardings littered the landscape like icons in an Orthodox church, selling the virtues of fizzy drinks and canned food. Then we found a new art form, the decorated petrol station: some sculpted like aeroplanes hovering above the pumps; Others like the back drop to a stage play, painted and decorated often in the colours of the Yemeni flag – red, white and black. There were blacksmiths welding gates which were usually blue because we were told, it repelled flies and the evil eye.

Kites and vultures wheeled above us. Clusters of bee-hives stood by the roadside. Naji was hungry.

'A day without meat is like a day without driving,' he said, grinning and tapping a cigarette between his fingers.

We were still driving along open plains dotted with clusters of buildings when we stopped to dine at the Al Jamali restaurant, open to the outside with three walls and an overhead fan. Naji did his usual trick and rushed into the kitchens, while we washed our hands. A small aluminium dish arrived with saffron rice, curried potato and a little spaghetti. This was followed by a spicy hot pepper, garlic and turmeric dish, with tomatoes and lamb. Naji looked critically at the rice. To some tribesmen in Yemen rice is seen as inferior to sorghum, wheat and barley. He began shouting.

'What's the matter now?' said Charles.

'He's complaining that someone in the restaurant is the son, father and mother of a donkey because they don't clean the tables,' was Ahmed's reply.

After clearing a table we all tucked into the food in silence and finished off with a sweet Tihaman coffee. Naji was horrified if anyone drank while they ate.

'You must drink afterwards – otherwise it is bad for your stomach,' he said.

We were only 16 kilometres from Hodeidah, and drove along a straight road, sucking us into the distance through endless expanses of sand. Then we came upon a police check.

'Why is there a police check here?' asked Charles.

'In case we have firearms.'

Hodeidah is Yemen's fourth largest city. It felt as though we were in another Yemen. The sea itself is the natural resource of the city. The port had been built by the Russians and was the busiest in Yemen. All about us were modern concrete structures, architecturally undistinguished, borrowing influences from countries that had lost their culture and traditions. To some who arrive from the medieval fortresses of the highlands the city is a breath of fresh air with its use of twentieth-century building techniques and designs, straight parallel streets and shiny new restaurants. To me it was a cacophony of design but like all ill-built cities had the potential to surprise you with its people.

We arrived at the Hotel Bristol in the early afternoon. The hotel was one of very few places in the whole of Yemen where you could buy beer easily, and our throats were parched. Having quenched our thirst we went to our rooms for an afternoon nap. The electricity was off, which happens regularly in Yemen, so there was no air conditioning.

Our Nikon camera seemed to have given up in the heat. The covering of the Hasselblad had already melted and the metal of our film cassettes was hot to the touch. We left the film in a cool bag while we took the Nikon out to do a test strip, and process the film.

Just a stone's throw away from the hotel stood a photographer's. 'Salem Studios' was written in big red and yellow letters across the front of the shop. What a godsend, we thought. Most of Yemen is made up of remote villages – it was just as well the camera had broken down here, where we could test it. Charles bought a film and went into the street and photographed anything that passed in front of us, at different shutter speeds and with different apertures to check that everything worked. A small crowd gathered around Ahmed as he watched us. He began laughing.

'What is the problem?' asked Charles.

'They want to know why you are photographing the noisy traffic and why don't you photograph the sunset or the sea, or something similar.' It seemed a good idea and we left our film to be processed and drove down to the corniche that swept around the edge of Hodeidah. The wind was blowing furiously.

'One good thing about the wind is that it takes the mosquitoes away,' said Ahmed 'They are too delicate to fly in these conditions!'

We looked at the Red Sea rippling in front of us. The nets of fish traps were strung out in the water. Rows of smart black four-wheel-drives were parked nearby, as if they had recently arrived by sea. Couples strolled romantically along the beach, in a manner unseen in the mountainous regions. Children hurried in and out of the cool water while their mothers, seemingly untroubled by the problems of the world strolled up and down the corniche with large ice creams. This was a different Yemen, where people were more relaxed with their families out of doors. In the mountains much of the communal activity in towns, particularly between men and women is kept inside the house.

We returned to 'Salem Studios' and picked up our film. Everything about the camera seemed to be in order, we were relieved.

'It's time to eat fish,' announced Ahmed. 'The Mahdi Restaurant is the oldest fish restaurant in Hodeidah, let's eat there.' Naji protested, but Ahmed was by the coast and insisted.

We parked in the centre of town, not far from the sea. A wedding party passed us in the street, horns beeping in celebration.

The Mahdi Restaurant was old, as Ahmed had said and it was run by a man who was even older. Bent double and moving slowly, he welcomed us in and dusted some chairs for us to sit on. The room was large, a little like a transport cafe – fluorescent tubes, plastic tables and ceramic tiles; everything that should produce an evening out devoid of atmosphere. But strangely it was full of character. Naji rushed into the kitchen.

'He can't surely be checking the meat in a fish restaurant,' said Charles.

'He walks into every place as if he was a member of the family,' said Ahmed raising his hands. 'Everywhere we go people come up and greet him.'

We were led to a large, deep fridge to choose our fish. Ahmed plunged in his hands.

'We want the best fish,' he said and we sat down again.

Ten minutes later the fish was brought to each of us on an Arabic newspaper. It had been cooked in a tandoor – with paprika, spices and garlic. We tore off pieces beneath the charred, flaky skin. The white flesh tasted even better than it smelled. Using our fingers we feasted on delicious bread, fine and fluffy – cooked in ghee, like a light pastry. Naji brought us a blood-red spicy sauce, and we found out he had once again been doubling up as a chef in the kitchen, protecting our stomachs and making sure everything was fresh.

'This is the rough sea season; storms build up and not much fish is caught out to sea. So it is a little more expensive than usual,' said Ahmed. When we went to pay, Naji complained about the outrageously high price and then haggled over it.

'No, they are not tourists!' he shouted, 'they are friends from my house.' The man at the till backed off a little as Naji waved his hands at him. As we left, a poor man came up to our table asking for our left-overs – of which there were many on Naji's plate. Fish to Naji was childrens' food. The poor man took the plate and sat at a nearby table. The man at the till walked over to him and gave him five of our riyals.

Even though it was late we found some local qat sellers for Ahmed and Naji. Perhaps people in Hodeidah did a decent day's work before they chewed. Nearby stalls sold melons, and vegetables. The only concession to tradition here were some terracotta pots, and incense jars with designs dating back 2,000 years.

At night Hodeidah market was lit up with hurricane lamps, like a scene from the nineteenth century, which changed the atmosphere completely. The qat market stood on open ground – small huddles of people all crouched arguing prices. In nearby stalls hurricane lamps lit up dates and grapes, reflecting off their waxy surfaces. Yet the reality of globalisation had arrived in Hodeidah for nearly everything manufactured seemed to be imported. Plastic hangers with childrens' clothes and plastic toys from China. Plastic buckets, plastic trays and plastic cassette covers, all under plastic tarpaulin. Metal suitcases that looked as if they had come from India, and metal pots. The shoes probably from the Far East, all piled high.

We had exhausted the streets.

'I could die for some tea,' I said.

'You probably will – the water here is terrible for drinking,' said Ahmed. 'Really terrible. In Sana'a, Aden and Taiz it is good for drinking. There is one good tea shop I know about, so let's go there.'

The Bin Yaseen tea shop had two large blue plywood tables outside in the street. We sat at one and watched the owner throw water on the ground to keep down the dust. Soon a metal tray arrived – tea with milk, nutmeg and sugar, served in a well used glass on a green china saucer. A man at the next table leaned towards us. He had pale green eyes. All over Yemen you can find people with distinctive green eyes – perhaps a Turkish trait.

'Everyone in Hodeidah comes here to drink. They serve the best tea here. Where are you from?' he asked.

'Scotland.' replied Charles.

'Oh, north of England.'

'That's right.'

'I used to live in Aden, when the British were there. But I had to escape after the British left in 1967.'

Many people left Aden when the British left, fleeing the communists, many were northerners anyway. Some, including important merchants, came to Hodeidah, others went further inland to Taiz or Sana'a and over a period of thirty years became integrated.

'What was it like?' I asked.

'Oh Aden was before like Beirut was in the 1970s, beautiful!' he said. 'Now it's terrible – Hodeidah better.'

'Why is that?'

'The government that replaced Britain took everything – shops, homes, everything. I like the British – my sister lives in England – but she is too fat! When the British left Aden, I went to Taiz. Now we are becoming a democratic country. Everything has changed, let's hope we have a future. There is plenty of the past in Yemen. What we need is a future!'

* * *

It was Friday, the day Beit al-Faqih a little way along the coastal plain had its main market. The inevitable motorcycles with their silencers removed went futt-futt-futt along the road. The stretch from Hodeidah to the market was as straight as a ruler, and newly asphalted. 'A sand storm is brewing,' said Ahmed, re-adjusting himself in his seat. 'Definitely a sand storm.'

Vehicles veered everywhere. Goats and sheep piled high in the backs of Toyota trucks, swayed as they passed us. The road was fast disappearing under a blizzard of sand the colour of fired pottery with the heat of a kiln. It blew around with unabated fury as we motored to the market.

Ahmed was happy this morning – brought up by the coast in Aden he had loved the fish last night. Naji, a highland Yemeni, was not in his best mood – no meat yesterday, too much driving, and the heat was getting to him.

The mood in the car was apprehensive. Storms in the Tihama at such high summer temperatures were no laughing matter. We stopped along the road and bought a couple of litres of cold bottled water and drank it all immediately. The sun was rising high in the sky and the heat was oppressive.

The town of Beit al-Faqih – the 'House of the Sage', was named after Ahmed bin Musa bin Ujayl, a scholar of the late thirteenth century famous for his wisdom and sanctity. When the German explorer Carsten Niebuhr visited in 1763 he wrote that traders from as far afield as India, Morocco, Persia and even Europe did business here.

'I want to stop to take a photograph,' I said. 'Naji pull over please.'

Naji once again carefully took the vehicle to the side of the road.

I gathered my camera bag and took out a Nikon 80-200mm lens. It was so hot that it burnt my hands. As I left the vehicle the wind blew my hair into my eyes and sand all over me. I could taste it in my mouth. I felt a mess. I began to understand why so many women in Yemen were happy to be covered up. I threw my scarf over my face and the camera to protect both.

This must be one of the most interesting markets in the Arabian Peninsula. Japanese vehicles were arriving laden with bleating sheep, while a throng of white turbaned men, in fine linen, courteously vacated the space in front of me. These were men who for generations had herded, farmed and fished, or learned a specialist craft to support their families in this harsh landscape. Through the lens of my camera, I could see from their faces that they were enjoying trading together. Just visible in the distance motorbikes sped by, overtaking the slow, graceful oxen being driven to market. A last gasp of wind blew me back into the vehicle.

'Oh my God! – look at you,' screamed Ahmed.

'I looked into the rearview mirror. You might have thought someone had thrown an egg over me, followed by a bucket of sand.

We moved on. We passed stalls displaying all sorts of delicacies – breads and Arab sweets. No wonder Yemen has been called the 'breadbasket of Arabia.' The Greek geographer, Ptolemy called Southern Arabia, 'Arabia Emporium' – 'Arabian Market', because of its many markets and the reputation of its people from earliest times as great traders. We wanted to find the house of some of Yemen's best known hand-weavers, and knew it was close. Ahmed called to a passer-by.

'Hey, can you tell me where the weavers live?'

'Go straight, take a left and continue, you'll see them soon enough.'

'I'm feeling lost already,' said Ahmed.

Naji edged forward through the market which had a sense of superb organisation in a state of chaos. We sat in silence watching him weave a path through the crowds like Moses parting the Red Sea. We passed great lengths of rope, basket makers, terracotta pots, containers of dried fish, spices, grain, and henna sold by women. Delicacies of all kinds were on sale, deep-fried batter and griddle cakes, muffins, scones, sweets made from dates, sesame seeds and honey.

Leaving the market we made our way through a series of small narrow alleyways between buildings of concrete, coral and mud.

Many of these one-storey houses were very beautifully built, often with walled gardens, and had highly decorative stucco façades suggestive of Indian and Persian influences.

In a small compound, away from the main market, we found the family of weavers. Ahmed spoke with them for a few minutes explaining that we wanted to photograph the process and some of the cloth.

'They say they are the last family weaving cloth in Beit al-Faqih,' said Ahmed turning to us, 'come with me.' Ahmed led us along the side of a white wall and into a shady courtyard roofed with loose beams letting shafts of light on to the floor. It reminded me of a temporary room for the Passover. There were three looms. At the far edge by a wall, two elderly lean men, stripped to the waist, sat at either end of the loom, throwing a ball of red cotton at each other, as if playing some kind of entrancing game. The method of weaving is ancient and the cloth is produced in multicoloured stripes, using locally grown cotton and – rarely these days – silk. The most common colours are black, yellow, red and white, but blues and greens are also used, reminding me of the great bands of sand, salt and sea which dominate the coastline of the Tihama.

'A reasonably sized piece of cloth can take between four to six days to produce, using designs passed down between families, 'said Ahmed. 'They say the cloth is guaranteed for one hundred years.'

Yemeni cloth has been famous since the time of Mohammed, who is said to have been wrapped in it before burial. During the lifetime of the Prophet it is also claimed that the Kaaba in Mecca was covered in it. In the eleventh century the Persian traveller Nasir-i Khusrau wrote of the textiles in Sana'a that 'her striped coats, stuffs of silk and embroideries have the greatest reputation.' Until recently indigo was famously made in Yemen, especially in the villages of the Tihama. A few remote homes in Yemen still make indigo using local stamps to identify the supplier, but the craft is cherished and I was told by one market stall holder who sold me some it was kept a secret.

I think the fish harbour in Hodeidah is one of the great spectacles of the Arabian Peninsula. Local boats leave here to return laden with anything from fragile shrimps so small it takes hundreds to fill a small woven basket, to plump-bellied sharks, so heavy fishermen can hardly manoeuvre them around the concrete jetty. The atmosphere is frantic with activity. Wheelbarrows loaded with fish race past while fish are dragged, pulled, and strung up. Groups of men looked on astonished at each other's catches; one brightly coloured lobster caused great interest, paraded on the bonnet of a Toyota truck. A fish oil smell pervaded the air, reminding us of the days before prepackaging sanitised the life out of our food.

The old Turkish quarter, a few hundred yards away, proclaims Hodeidah's past prosperity as an entrepot of Red Sea trade. Now rubbish and debris are strewn across earthen alleyways, once elegant buildings are crumbling like cake. Half-naked children play with toy carts, while women cast quick glances through cracks in doorways. Its glory has faded, but, beneath the peeling paint, rusting door hinges, fallen plasterwork and masonry, breathed the spirit of the Ottomans. As we wandered along narrow footpaths, we saw highly carved window boxes and lintels on every house. It was reminiscent of Old Jeddah, or some far-off place like Zanzibar.

One building in particular caught our attention for its intricate carvings around the window frames. An office occupied the ground floor, in which two white-shirted men sat at desks. They could have been administrators transported straight from India during the British period. Neatly-piled files and books surrounded them in a bare, brightly-painted room, open to the street.

We were beckoned over.

'You like the house?' said one of the men nodding and smiling.

'Yes the carvings are extraordinary,' I replied.

'You haven't seen anything yet, upstairs is beautifully decorated. You want to visit upstairs?' he said rising from his seat and pointing in the direction of the door.

'Is it possible to see inside?' I asked Ahmed, looking up to a set of wooden shutters on the outside of the building.

Ahmed spoke to them in Arabic. One of the men put his arm out towards a corridor to encourage us to move forward. We walked around a corner up some steps into a small courtyard. In front of us was a door painted brilliant blue. I looked at the rubbish the wind had piled up outside and realised it had not been opened for months.

The man produced a large old rusty key and unlocked the door. Then he pushed. The doors swung open and he flung his hands out in front of him as if to push the dust away. He then led us through a verandah door into a large white room. It was magical.

We slipped momentarily into the past. All around us were small niches, of Mughal design, set into the walls. Between the niches were mirrors, and above them painted peacocks strutting in all their finery. As we looked across the room the man threw open another door. We walked through into a second room. The room was divided into two by heavily varnished wooden panels inset with yellow, blue, red and green glass, some resembling Victorian pressed glass. A blaze of colour reminiscent of a Byzantine church lit up the floor, with a jewel-like quality. Decorative stucco-work graced the upper parts of the walls.

We were told the house was originally owned by the Al-Jebeli family, who were native to Hodeidah.

'They were merchants – agents and distributors to the King, Imam Ahmed.' said our companion in a tone of nostalgia. 'They traded in tobacco, animal leather, salt, and coffee between Aden and Hodeidah. Then later the house was bought by Mohammed Ali Hassan.'

We photographed the interior and went back on to the rubble of the streets, leaving this small gem to be closed to the wider world once again.

It was time to move on. We found a petrol station and sat watching two people smoking while re-filling their cars.

'This country is in the hands of God,' said Ahmed as he looked towards them.

Naji was outside, checking the oil and water. His shirt dripped with perspiration. He poured the contents of a cold water-bottle over his head, soaking his clothes and turned to speak to a boy nearby.

'I've been in a Turkish bath and I know what it's like. It is like this place. You lot might as well live in a Turkish bath.'

'Well, it is a little warm' said the boy.

'Warm? This is death itself.' Naji bellowed back. Like most modern Arabs he did not really like the heat.

'But we are used to it!' shouted the boy skipping away.

As we sat Ahmed noticed an advertisement for Canada Dry.

'This is the reason I ran away to Canada,' he said laughing. Ahmed started talking about his life in Aden as a child and how he left when the British went.

'When the British left Aden, I didn't know where to go. I wasn't going to stay there. But in Aden they kept advertising 'Drink Canada Dry' so I thought I would!'

Ahmed explained how he had studied sociology at university and then travelled, getting whatever jobs he could. He talked of being abroad and free to roam.

'There was a TV commercial in Canada,' said Ahmed, 'it said 'If you have a dream, come to us, and we will realise it together.' So I took my money out of the Royal Trust and put it in the Bank of Montreal.'

'And did you make your dream?' asked Charles.

'No I lost all my money!' Ahmed fell about laughing.

He stayed there for nine years. Failed relationships eventually brought him back, and he had not seen his family for many years. We are all born into a tradition, sometimes to step outside it is painful. It was the conflict of the modern world versus old values, that all good thinkers today ultimately have to come to terms with.

'My family didn't know where I was so I decided to return to my father's village, here in Yemen. Six weeks later I married.'

We drove north out of Hodeidah, towards Hajjah, a mountain stronghold which we hoped to reach before nightfall. After about twenty minutes, Ahmed raised his hands in the air and gasped.

'Its incredible! Naji saw a stone coming from a car, before it even hit the windscreen. He put his hand up in front of his eye, in case it broke the glass and hit his face.'

I had already noticed that Yemenis have eyes like hawks. For people living in cities, acute powers of sight are no longer essential. I am certain Yemenis can see much further and more clearly than most people. Perhaps it is something to do with genes, bred out in the desert and treacherous mountain ranges, where to notice a slight movement or subtle change can be the difference between life and death. This ability is also present in their reading of the human psyche. Yemenis notice immediately the moment your mood changes.

They sense things, and it is difficult to hide your emotions when you are with them, as they pick up the slightest change in attitude. Many people in the villages are illiterate, but intelligent. They socialise together and therefore quickly read the human mind. Although very independent people, they also appreciate and acknowledge the importance of their group, and the knowledge that people influence one another. This is one reason Naji never liked any of us falling asleep when he was driving. 'If you fall asleep, I will fall asleep.' Naji kept saying – and we didn't want that – so awake we all stayed.

We left the main road and headed west down Wadi Mawr towards Al-Luhayya. Here the road was rougher, in parts the gravel was as sharp as knives. The landscape was flat – seemingly endless miles of sand and scrub. Camels grazed amongst cacti, cattle egrets perched precariously on their backs.

The most notable element of the landscape were the small settlements of houses and workshops. These were not the great defensive structures of the highlands but thatched huts, mostly circular, sometimes oblong, grouped in walled or fenced compounds. Stone is rather rare; instead the craftsman's expertise lies in using grasses, reeds, palms and wetted earth as a binder. The whole structure is tied down by a rope system. Each hut, a single room, is set aside for a different purpose, sleeping quarters, a kitchen, storage, and animals.

We stopped just before Al Mutarid, and parked in the shade of a lone tree. I wanted to see whether it was possible to take some photographs of these refined handmade structures. A man came up to greet us as we climbed out of the Toyota. He saw our cameras and indicated to us that we were welcome to visit. A few chickens rushed in front of us next to a tethered donkey, a young girl wrapped in purple cotton with a yellow head-scarf followed us in. We were shown to the main room. It was light, but surprisingly cool. A few wooden beds, carved with a simple cross-hatch design, stood neatly around the perimeter. Above us, on the ceiling, was a magical painting in bright abstract forms with a mixture of iconography from everyday life – a car, an aeroplane, even a tank with guns; the panoply of Tihama life and imagination marked out here like an aboriginal dreamtime sequence. Enamelled plates and mirrors, to ward off evil spirits we were told, hung on carefully placed wooden pegs.

The children ran over to us and Naji started chasing them and telling them to get out of the way. A man came up shaking his head in time with his finger and said 'Why do you shout at the children like this?'

'Because they are spoiling the picture,' replied Naji. 'They come running over here like cats.'

'Don't say this about children,' came the reply. 'They are one hundred percent human beings.'

We wanted to move on to the coast, but the heat was appallingly uncomfortable, a savage dust storm blocked Naji's view of the road and blotted out the sun. Sand invaded every corner of the Landcruiser and the plastic surfaces on both our cameras was melting. We had only nibbled at the edge of the Tihama, but to go any further on this visit would not help us, there were no old retired British-Yemeni seamen in these parts and the heat was ruining our photography and film stock. We needed to move to higher ground.

The road to Shaharah

Wadi Lissam

The Wild West of Arabia

'I was wise once, I cried when I was born.'
(Welsh proverb)

Naji alighted from the vehicle. He uttered a rapid series of words in Arabic.

'What is it this time?' asked Charles.

'Another puncture, another nail,' replied Ahmed.

'Another nail?' repeated Charles. 'You seem to have so many, perhaps you should start mining them.'

'Yes we'll do a feasibility study,' laughed Ahmed. It was the third puncture in two days.

Our destination was Shaharah. We had driven from Hajjah, another town situated on top of a dramatic mountain range above the source of Wadi Mawr. We stopped at Huth, on the main road between Sana'a and Sadah. We were in the region of the Hashid and the Bakil, the two largest tribal confederations in the northern Yemeni highlands. The village is particularly interesting architecturally, with lofty rectangular stone tower houses rising out of the plateau. It should have warned us we were entering a region of people with strong attitudes. There are some interesting mosques in the village. In fact in the past Huth was to Sana'a as Aberdare in the Welsh Valleys was to Cardiff – known for its education, and sons of religion. But with our arts and geological background, both Charles and I were more interested in the immediate visual and photographic potential of the town. People here were not used to visitors and we left quite quickly, heading west. The Landcruiser stopped yet again. Patiently Naji changed the tyre but he was obviously concerned at having to drive through this remote tribal area with a car problem.

'They call this area the 'Wild West' of Arabia,' said Ahmed smiling.

We continued for a few miles more until we found a rusty shack – a small garage workshop. It was drenched in oil, and tall pillars of used tyres lay outside. Naji was in heaven.

Across the road stood a beautiful but run-down two-storey house. Faded and flaking paint in blue, green and yellow reminded me of a Pompeii mural and it seemed a promising photograph.

As I took my camera across the road two tribesmen came over.

'Stop! Stop!' shouted one of them.

'What now?' said Charles.

Ahmed moved towards the men, raising his hand.

'Stop! Stop!' the man continued. 'It is not good to take pictures of this house. It is not a good house, it is a mess. It is against the Koran to take such pictures.'

Ahmed was annoyed at this. An awkward silence followed.

'Well who is responsible for the house being in such a mess then?' retorted Ahmed.

'It's none of your business, just don't take pictures.' His expression was serious.

'What good Muslim would leave his house in such an unsightly state? Anyway the woman here likes the colours on the wall, and has seen something positive about the house.'

I thought Ahmed was getting too close to the bone on the subject. The price you pay for saying or doing the right thing is so often unpopularity. In this remote place where everyone carried guns was it worth it?

For the next fifteen minutes, while Naji had the tyres off his Landcruiser, we were hostage to our newly-found friends. Ahmed, a skilled diplomat, spoke with the man who complained that I was not wearing a headscarf. Ahmed never raised his voice but told him plainly that I had a right to wear what I wanted. 'What if someone came and asked you to veil your wife or daughter?'

The statement, I thought, would have annoyed all the right people. They debated the issue, then Ahmed, who was very self controlled, asked authoritatively; 'Does the Koran recognise Moses and Jesus?'

'Yes,' replied the man, whose dogma was now being reinforced.

'Well these people are followers of Christ, so let us respect them.'

The man was astonished that Ahmed spoke to him in such a frank way. Jesus enjoys a special place in Islam, he is one of the six greatest prophets: – Adam, Noah, Abraham, Moses, Jesus and Mohammad – and is mentioned in fifteen suras and ninety-three verses. Without faltering, Ahmed returned to the Toyota. Out of his bag came a copy of Sheikh Said's letter, from the South Wales Islamic Centre. In it Sheikh Said explained how many Yemenis had come to settle in Wales, and were happy living there, amongst the local people. Many had married in Cardiff and some of the women had converted to Islam. Of course the prophet Mohammed himself had had a Christian wife and there is a special place for 'people of the book', as the three monotheistic faiths share a common faith in one God. It is recognised that before God's revelation to Muslims via the Prophet Mohammed, God had used the Bible to reveal himself to Christians and Jews and it is part of a Muslim's mission to debate about God with them. In fact, not far from where we were standing was possibly one of the earliest venues of inter-faith dialogue. In 630 a Christian delegation from Najran – then part of Yemen, on the Saudi border – went to Medina to discuss the importance of Christians co-existing with the Muslim community.

'God be with you!' cried the man in a loud voice.

As a country where just about everyone accepts that God exists, and is in control, Yemen is blessed. It is a moving experience to travel somewhere where the thought of life without God is, for most people, unthinkable. Yemenis are proud that they accepted Islam voluntarily very early in the seventh century. They were amongst the first to convert to Islam and their troops played a critical part in the expansion of the Islamic Empire. From Yemen also came religious scholars, and those deeply committed to the advancement of science and the arts.

There was no stopping our new friends now. Ahmed could not get a word in edge-ways.

'He is inviting us to go and chew qat with them, they want to discuss more about this,' said Ahmed laughing. Ahmed had triumphed. In Yemen a person who can solve a problem in society is valued greatly.

'We are sorry, but we have to reach Shaharah by dusk.'

The men looked towards the Blue Mountains and thunderous sky. 'By dusk? You had better get on your way with God's blessing.'

We moved off, the four-wheel-drive skating across the flat sandy landscape. We meditated on our chance meeting. John Bunyan would have enjoyed it and I thought of Ahmed's patience. The patience of Job (Ayyub) – who in this land is believed to have been a Yemeni.

A few minutes later Ahmed turned around and spoke.

'In this area, I think you should consider putting on a head scarf.'

This was the first time Ahmed has suggested such a thing, so I took it seriously. I had bought a black chiffon scarf edged with red from a women in Al Hajjarah and put it on.

As we drove across Wadi Lissam, the agriculture became richer, with fruit orchards, green fields and groves of palm trees casting lengthy shadows. It looked like the Garden of Eden. The landscape changed to more open ground and we passed a woman carrying a container of water on her head and another two women with a donkey. They were wearing flat straw hats interwoven with purple strands. In this remote place they looked like South Americans.

Then the thunder came, first a rumble; then the sky became overcast.

After about an hour we reached a small village at the base of the mountain. A few young people were jacking a battered old vehicle up on to blocks. Welding equipment, pumps and cans, were strewn everywhere. In such a rural place such industry seemed out of place. It had the semblance of kinetic art, without the gallery.

'There is Shaharah!' exclaimed Ahmed gesturing towards a distant point on the top of the mountain. It looked like a long way away. Dusk was approaching. Kawkaban seemed a mere pimple in comparison.

A discussion ensued between Ahmed, Naji and a local youth who was to drive us up to Shaharah. We were ushered in to a nearby Toyota pick-up truck. Naji explained he was staying down in the valley to 'protect the vehicle'. Ahmed suggested we sat in the back of the open vehicle. The driver, Mahmood Hassan threw the last remaining wheel from a nearby vehicle into the back where we were sitting. A small boy, no older than seven, bent down to pump up our tyres, while an elderly man shuffled over and began securing the latch on the tail-gate on which we were leaning. Naji then turned to Mahmood and told him if rain came, he was not to continue the journey but get us accommodation in a local house, half way up.

'It will take about two hours,' said Ahmed. 'The normal road is closed for repairs. We have to go up an ancient route. It will be a demanding journey.'

The storm was still brewing. Shaharah lies at 3,000 metres. It is a village divided between the mountains of Jebel Al Amir, and Jebel Al Feesh and joined by a unique and ancient bridge. This bridge was the reason we were going there. Mahmood, we found out, was a self taught driver, seventeen years of age, married, and already a father of two. A *jambia* slung below his waist, he was armed with a Kalashnikov, and his smile revealed a mouth full of green qat. We took one look at him, and the local terrain, and realised that Ahmed had been right, when he had said that we had entered the 'Wild West' of Yemen. Mahmood indicated he was ready and jumped behind the wheel. He started up the engine and lit a cigarette. It was his second trip that day. Ahmed, who sat next to Mahmood, looked back at us, and with a wink and a nod, crossed his fingers in the air – an ancient Christian sign against the evil eye – and then grasped the dashboard.

In front of us appeared a sheer rock face. Mahmood prepared the engine for our ascent. The pick-up struggled to keep a grip on the steep track as pieces of limestone were ground between rock and rubber, shooting out from beneath the tyres as we lurched up the mountain. I felt my pulse quicken. I could already see the reason that Shaharah was well known for vehicles with double layered tyres – a piece of rock could easily rip through one skin.

There was no road as such, just a grey-green rock surface. We gripped the tail-gate and looked up into the emptiness of the sky. We were leaning backwards. Mahmood held the vehicle on the road by turning the wheel constantly – right, then left and right again.

The thunder now alternated with bursts of lightning. It was as if a great battle was being fought above us. The clouds darkened even more as the sun slid behind the mountain.

Our journey lasted a full two hours, one in near darkness, another lit by the lightning bursts. As we approached Shaharah our route was paved like a Roman Road. It had been a forbidding journey and was interrupted only by the occasional stalling of the engine and hairpins too tight to drive around in one movement, where we had to edge back and forth on the lip of a thousand foot drop, before we could complete the turn and continue.

'You are a better Muslim now, and we are better Christians!' I said to Ahmed when we reached the top.

'Well now I can tell you. Two vehicles recently left the road here and fell down the cliff, but the Germans sitting in the back escaped. That's why I put you in the back.' It was so like Ahmed.

Our *funduq* was a medieval castle now bathed in moonlight. A veiled young woman greeted us. With the energy of a young gazelle, she led us up four flights of steep stone stairs into the *mafraj* – a large room which we were all to share.

We woke early. The early morning light cast a warm ochre glow over the stone village – extravagant dashes of white paint highlighted the windows. Shaharah was once an important fortress town – but much of its population has left since the 1960s civil war. Jagged mountains dropped away into the distance around us. The scene was breathtaking.

Ahmed suddenly pointed towards a woman collecting fodder for her animals on the edge of a cliff directly across from where we were sitting. We all sat mesmerised as she moved cautiously towards a tuft of green grass on the edge of the mountain. Below her was what must have been a huge drop. She pulled her long black dress above her hips and tucked it into a belt, revealing billowing black trousers as she sank down on to the rocky ground. She seemed to be risking her life in her eagerness to gather good fodder. We all froze.

Our attention was diverted by the girl who had greeted us the night before, who entered the room with a tray of sweetly spiced tea and bread, revealing only her eyes and pale hands. Stepping over my mattress, on to a window ledge, she sat quietly watching us eat. After a few minutes she pulled a leaflet out from a pocket, pointed to a travel poster on the wall, and began speaking rapidly, addressing Ahmed. She stood up, took the poster off the wall and moved towards him.

'This is her picture,' said Ahmed handing the brochure to me. 'A Frenchman took it eight years ago when she was twelve years old.'

I looked at the cover, her deep dark eyes were like sunken treasure.

She was the epitome of innocence, so loved by the French.

'It has been a cover for some time now. She is worried that her picture is on the front of one of the travel brochures,' he said. 'She will soon be married and her husband will not be pleased that her face is seen by the world. Before she gets married she has to convince the company to change the brochures.'

'Many Yemenis say it is not important that women in much of the country are shrouded in black,' continued Ahmed. 'They can tell what a woman is like from the type of material she chooses. The way the veil is worn. The gracefulness of a movement. How a women looks after her hands or the type of shoes she wears. A woman's personality can be revealed despite the veil. The eyes tell everything.'

Charles and I finished the bread and tea, and I took my camera to the window. The woman was still foraging on the cliff's edge. Mahmood came into the room and sat down, although he was eager to get going. I turned my camera towards him, asking if I could take his photograph. He agreed and sat up on his knees. The image of a tribal Yemeni, gun in hand, at ease with himself and the world, had an immediate appeal.

The girl who had been sitting close at hand, beckoned to me.

'Photo?' she said. I was surprised, after the concerns which she had expressed to Ahmed. She sat back on the window-ledge. I positioned myself, steadied the camera and began to focus. She put out her hand towards Mahmood, uttering a few words. He threw his Kalashnikov over to her. She caught it perfectly, and grasping it firmly between her fingers sat bolt upright. I looked at her sitting in the window, and felt puzzled. With Ahmed she had been worried about a picture of herself looking young, innocent and unveiled. Now she had chosen to be photographed veiled, but holding a gun. I took the picture quickly then returned to the window – still worried about the woman on the cliff. She had collected her grass, and was moving to safer ground.

We now visited the extraordinary bridge that straddled a deep gorge between the two mountains. Built in the seventeenth century by the architect Saleh al-Yamani, it was constructed from tough lime-stone blocks, and is quite an engineering achievement.

Here Charles too perched himself on the edge of the cliff to get the classic photograph. He did this with surprising calm, only to be assailed by nervousness, at the thought of actually crossing it. After all, just underneath it, could be seen the remains of two previous bridges that had collapsed.

The journey down the mountain was no less arduous than the ascent, except for the strong sun that beat down upon our heads. It felt as if we were slipping off the edge of the world. About half way down we heard what sounded like a gunshot. It was another burst tyre. We stopped, and Ahmed and Mahmood changed it.

Naji was relieved to see us and eager to leave, which we did almost immediately.

'This area, crazy people,' said Naji, looking across at some men he had spent the night with. He settled back into his seat and headed at full speed back to Huth on the main road. Here we stopped at a little roadside restaurant for lunch: soup, *helba*, fried eggs and tomatoes.

Our road now headed northwards to the old mud city of Sadah. We passed vast irrigated fields, dotted with stone watchtowers and shepherd's huts with vaulted ceilings. At times volcanic vistas with cones and limestone pavements, replaced farmland. Beside the road, we came across houses painted with red and white stripes. As we stopped to take some pictures, two men arrived, swinging their Kalashnikovs around their shoulders. They skipped across the asphalt road and questioned us as to what we were doing in these parts.

'They are protecting the area,' Ahmed whispered. 'It's like old Texas here.'

One of the men was about twenty years old with long black hair in ringlets. He was blind in one eye, his teeth were misshapen and he was shabbily dressed. Naji became visibly fidgety. I explained in broken Arabic, that I was interested in the markings on a nearby house and I wandered off, passing an old woman and some children playing on the ground near a well. All the houses were two storeys high, and had reddish-orange stripes resembling the pattern on a honey-bee. Minutes later Ahmed came to find me.

'Hurry, get back to the vehicle.'

'Why what is the matter?'

'The tribes around here have been fighting. One man was shot in the leg by another tribe, and they have to do the same in retaliation. They are waiting for a vehicle to pass.'

'What! Those two men with Kalashnikovs?

'Yes, they are serious.'

'Are you sure?'

'One of them has just told me. It's better that we leave. Even though the people here would not usually harm anyone. We have nothing to do with the tribal feud – but it does sometimes happen. We don't want a similar incident here. He's waiting to shoot someone. We mustn't hang around.'

'Are they fighting over land here?' I said.

'Here they fight over air.' Ahmed raised his hands in exasperation.

Guns have traditionally been used to solve local problems in tribal areas where efforts at mediation have failed.

If someone kills a member of your tribe it is a matter of honour to exact revenge. People in Yemen are well aware of the problems that can arise when there are so many weapons and educated towns people often look on the tribes as hopelessly savage. To a tribesman, ancestry and his independence are of paramount importance. He has to be generous, honourable, fierce but also fearless. Being distinct and different to a tribesman is crucial, even though he belongs to a group.

We hurried on towards Sadah, passing through mud village after mud village, many surrounded by walled vineyards. Historically the area had been inhabited by a large Jewish community, and the wine used by them was made here. A fleur-de-lys pattern, in moulded mud, decorated the outside walls of the houses. Noticing some goats that had climbed right up into an acacia tree, we stopped to photograph them. They were carefully balancing themselves on the thin branches. It was so quiet that even the silence was audible. Unexpectedly a shepherdess strolled through a cluster of bushes. She hadn't noticed us. In these more arid regions there is a greater reliance on herding sheep and goats. Throwing stones at her flock and whistling a hauntingly beautiful sound, she strolled across our field of view and disappeared into the distance. It was a moment when you realise that you are in a completely different world to your own.

Dusk came, and the sky darkened. Vehicles were passing us without lights, some driving down the middle of the road and some without even number plates.

'Too dangerous,' shouted Naji, getting exasperated. We were getting closer to the Saudi border, and an area known for smuggling, and lawlessness. We arrived in Sadah and booked into the local Al Mamoon Hotel. It was raining, and we were exhausted.

'You have brought a blessing with you,' I was told by the receptionist.

'In Britain if you arrive, and it is raining, they say you have brought bad weather with you!' I responded. Hailstones fell on the wrought-iron window bars tapping out a tune. We went upstairs, and slumped down on our beds for an hour before meeting downstairs for a meal.

Ahmed and Naji were watching the local television. Two men from the Far East were sitting on some large velvet-covered sofas. We guessed that they were Korean.

'You can't trust these Yemenis, they look nice to you and then when you turn your back – well!', shouted one of them across the room as we sat down.

'That's a bit hard,' said Charles pointing. 'Look at Ahmed, he's lovely.'

'Oh he may look lovely to you, but they can cause you problems. I have been in prison for one month.'

Charles turned to Ahmed and said 'Is he joking? Does he mean that being here is like being in prison?'

'No, he's serious.'

'Why did they put you in prison?' asked Charles.

'I was in prison because I drank liquor with Yemenis.'

'Now I know everything about Yemenis,' continued the Korean. 'There is nothing I do not know.' He laughed loudly. 'I have been in prison many times.'

I felt sorry for the man; he did not know how to find good friends or gain any trust. He just seemed to be floating through shallow experiences.

By the following morning the rain had subsided. We had heard that there was a village, Al Ghuraz not far away that was home to Jewish families known for their considerable skills as silversmiths. After winding our way past one vineyard after another, we arrived at the entrance to the village. It was a settlement of many tall houses made of *zabur*, a method of building using layers of mud with chopped straw. Ancient trees twisted and split, offered shade to darkly clad figures. We stopped beneath one house. Above us on an outside wall were prints made from covering a hand in blue paint and pressing it carefully around shuttered windows, to avert the evil eye and frighten off any spirit that might try to enter. Some young women, seeing me in the back of the vehicle, ran towards us. They immediately invited me to follow them into their house. I left Charles, Ahmed and Naji standing outside as I raced up the stairs leading to the roof. The view from the top leading across fields of vines with low-lying clouds of mist hovering mysteriously around the buildings was magical. I took some photographs of the girls who had brought me up to the top. Looking down on to the courtyard below, I could see my travelling companions deep in conversation, with a local man. A crowd of people had gathered and were clapping by the time I had scrambled down the stairs and was outside.

A man ran off to a nearby house.

'What's going on?' I asked

'He is bringing a letter that he has just been sent by one of his neighbours who emigrated to Boston in the USA,' replied Ahmed.

The man seemed troubled as he pressed the letter into Ahmed's hands.

Ahmed stood quietly reading its contents and then asked the man some questions. He turned to us.

'The man says a Jewish organisation in America came and convinced his neighbour that he would have a better life living in Boston. They organised his emigration. The letter is from his friend, now in Boston, who is Jewish remember,' said Ahmed, making direct eye contact with me. 'He regrets the day he left Al Ghuraz, and is waiting for the day that God will find him the money to return to Yemen. His best friend here is a Muslim, and he is very worried about him.'

'But that is terrible.' I said.

'Well there is nothing that can be done now. He sold his land.'

In Yemen Jewish people often associated themselves with a tribe and would be under their protection. Most of the villages in the tribal regions of Yemen, before 1948 would have had a small percentage of Jews. They owned land and sometimes had local Yemenis working for them, although they were most famous for their crafts.

Our interlocutor fetched grapes for us. He sent us off with his blessings, and thanked us for listening to his problem. We left feeling that ancient traditions of Jews and Muslims living happily together were being eroded by the myth of an easier life in the so called 'western world.'

Yemeni Jews have probably lived in Southern Arabia since pre-Islamic days. According to some historians five hundred Jewish archers arrived as part of the Roman army sent by Caesar Augustus and led by Aelius Gallus in 26 BC in an abortive attempt to conquer the Yemen. In the third quarter of the fourth century, the main ruling power in Yemen, the Himyarite dynasty under King Dhu Nuwas (518-525 AD), went as far as adopting Judaism as the state religion. How many locals actually followed the faith is unclear, but certainly it seems that it was practised by some, including the ruling classes, who had abandoned paganism. Later waves of Jewish immigrants arrived over the centuries, bringing valuable trading connections. Many came particularly through Aden, between the eleventh and thirteenth centuries, when it was an important link in east-west trade, with places such as Babylon, Syria, Egypt, India and Persia. Nearly half the population of Aden (some six hundred inhabitants) were Jewish when the British arrived in 1839. Although Christianity, and then Islam, emerged as the dominant faiths, the Jews have, throughout their history, been a crucial factor in the economy, arts and culture; despite periods of discrimination. Although they had to observe various Yemeni regulations, they have had an independent life for themselves, with their own traditions. The communities have been greatly depleted by the exodus in 1948 of at least 45,000 Jews, under 'Operation Flying Carpet', via British-controlled Aden to the newly established Israel. Today only a few hundred Jews are still left in Yemen.

We drove to the old walled city of Sadah, the most important trading centre in the far north of Yemen, only fifty miles from the Saudi border. A magnificent town wall, which has mostly survived in its sixteenth century layout, stretches around the old city. Although it was falling down due to disrepair, it was a splendid place from which to see panoramic views of the city, which is constructed entirely from mud – the distinctive *zabur* style. Overall responsibility for building a house here, like in many other parts of Yemen, is undertaken by a recognised builder who has served an apprenticeship. Earth, water and straw are trodden together on site for many hours, then shaped into balls by tossing them from hand to hand or pummelling them with a flat stick. Working in lines, the mixture is thrown from one person to the next, often to song. The soft beige colour of the houses, harmonising with the landscape, broken only by the plastered lime parapets and decorative bands of paint around windows and doors which strengthen the corners. Many of the buildings were in great need of repair, but still displayed a brooding, ageing beauty and dignity.

We continued to walk around the city walls. A man skipped by, wearing a pair of 1950s tortoise-shell glasses and a large *jambia*. He waved enthusiastically and pointed to the Great Mosque, which was hidden except for its massive minaret. Sadah has traditionally been a place where pilgrims to Mecca gather before crossing the border into Saudi Arabia, and it was at this spot they claim the prophet Mohammed's camel stopped for a rest.

We moved along to a better position to take some photographs. The Great Mosque has a unique series of twelve different sized and shaped domes, and a number of ancient tombs, dating back to the twelfth century. It is one of the outstanding structures of the town, and a legacy as much to sculpture as to architecture.

As a major religious centre, Sadah is known as the place at which the Zaydi Shi'ah Imamate was founded by Yahya ibn Hussain ibn Qasim ar-Rassi, or al Hadi ila al Haq (meaning 'the guide to the truth'). He was a sharif who came to Sadah from Medina on behalf of the Hamdam tribes. He left, only to return again in 897 AD to become an arbitrator, settling many regional problems caused by the fiercely independent tribes. At this time Sadah became the capital of the Zaydi state and home of the Zaydi Imams. Later they moved out to regions like Hajjah, Shaharah and Sana'a.

We walked down some steps nearby and wandered into the *suq*. A series of humble workshops below the wall are home to the last remaining Jewish silversmiths in the Arabian Peninsula. An array of silver horseshoe-shaped torques, armlets and anklets shone in the dim light. The joys and tribulations of Arabia can be read in much of the jewellery made to adorn the women. The designs and symbolisms are ancient, often superstitious or religious. Some pieces are worn as amulets to protect, others are inscribed with quotations from holy scripture. For the Bedouin, like their livestock, jewellery became a form of currency, often gained through trading. Aristocratic land-owning sections of society also needed jewellery, particularly for marriage dowries as an indication of a woman's personal wealth.

On a few low-lying tables lay bracelets, earrings, necklaces, and belts with their component chains, balls, bells and coins, some embellished with beaded wire. Coloured blue stones, worn as protection against the evil eye, set in silver. Warm tones of coral and amber, decorating other pieces. Yemeni jewellery is counted among the best quality in the Islamic World, and the recent decline of the craft is partly due to the emigration of the Jews to Israel. Al-Hamdani, the tenth-century Yemeni scholar wrote one of the oldest known treatises on the working techniques of precious metals.

The two jewellers sat on the floor chewing qat. Their handsome smiles revealed perfect shining white teeth. Two large black curled hair ringlets hung down at the side of their face.

'Are you German?' asked one.

'No British,' I replied.

'British? Not many British come here.'

'No,' I said.

'Are there Jewish people in Britain?.

'Yes many.'

'Do they wear their hair like ours?' he asked touching his curls and smiling.

'Some, mostly in London, but very few.'

'How many Jewish people are there in Britain, 4,000?' He stared straight at me waiting for an answer.

'I don't know.' I replied. I was later to find out it was a quarter of a million.

'How much is this?' I pointed to a finely worked bracelet, with a vine-leaf foliage motif, reminiscent of a pre-Islamic South Arabian frieze.

'Oh this piece is very nice, good silver. Very old. Nearly two hundred years.'

It looked very old, but of great quality in terms of workmanship and silver.

'Twenty dollars.' came the reply. I bought it immediately and as I left his workshop I tried to imagine what may have gone through the mind of the Yemeni-Jewish bride who had once proudly worn it.

Jewish silversmith, Sadah

Bedouin encampment, Ramalat as-Sabatayn

Let Them Eat Stones

'All that is best in the Arabs has come to them
from the desert'
(Wilfred Thesiger: *Arabian Sands*)

A bdul Karim sat on the hotel sofa, like a figure from an El Greco painting, draped in white, puffing a cigarette. Gesturing with his elegant hands, he spoke quickly in Arabic. He was going to be our *rafiq*, or guide, according to old Arab tradition, taking us across his tribal area, the scorching desert of the Ramlat as-Sabatayn, on the edge of the notorious Empty Quarter.

It was July, the hottest month of the year. We were in the ancient town of Marib, waiting to cross vast seas of sand to the Wadi Hadramaut, to photograph some of the most extraordinary mud architecture in the world. Our journey would take us through the desert where the authority of the Yemeni central government was scarcely felt. Oil had been discovered in the region in 1984.

'Abdul Karim says he was lost in the desert last week, for three days,' said Ahmed, cupping his ear and translating. Naji's eyebrows raised as he moved on to the edge of his seat and began to listen intently. Charles looked aghast. The last thing he wanted was to be lost in the desert, and part with three hundred dollars for the privilege. Ahmed slumped backwards, swallowed up by the armchair.

Abdul Karim's voice changed pitch.

'He's suggesting we take a different route to Shibam,' said Ahmed looking relieved. 'There have been ferocious sandstorms in the desert over the last month. He thinks we should avoid Shabwa. The route he is suggesting is a little shorter, but still a complete day by Landcruiser, unless something holds us up.'

'Or someone,' muttered Charles. 'Has he got a compass?' Charles liked to use one even in Britain.

Ahmed looked up at Abdul Karim and asked him.

'No he hasn't. Have you got one?' asked Ahmed turning his head towards Naji.

'No.' he replied, shrugging his shoulders.

'Then what will happen if we get lost?' Charles wanted to know.

Ahmed spoke to Abdul Karim again and then looked over to me.

'He says he carries tracer-tipped bullets for his Kalashnikov, that glow in the dark. He used them last week, and was found by some Bedouin.'

'Perhaps we ought to employ those Bedouin instead,' suggested Charles.

'But if we are to cross the desert safely, Abdul Karim says we must get going before day-break, while it is cool and get as far as possible before the sun rises. These Japanese vehicles are not like camels, they don't like the heat.'

We threw caution to the wind, and decided to go with Abdul Karim.

We left Abdul Karim, still smoking himself into an early grave, on the sofa and agreed to meet in two days, before walking out into the dark night with the sort of hope and optimism one needs on the edge of the Empty Quarter, resolving to find a shop that sold compasses, and to buy some extra provisions. Marib had the atmosphere of Bendigo or Ballarat during the Victoria gold rush. It now relied on new money made from servicing the oil industry nearby, and from a small amount of tourism.

'Tomorrow we go on a short excursion to the neighbouring village of Sirwah, before we try the desert crossing the following day.' said Ahmed. 'So let's get some rest and prepare, as it has not been safe there recently due to a tribal uprising. It's not very good to visit there at the moment.'

'It's no problem,' said Naji. 'We get guide.'

We returned to our room pondering on everything we had discussed. Naji went out to find a local who would travel with us to Sirwah.

We rose at dawn. Charles came out with some money and a medical kit.

'What is this?' said Naji.

'Medicine for my stomach,' I said.

'And in case we get shot,' said Charles wryly. 'I've also got money here in case the Bedouin kidnap Naji and we have to pay to get him back.'

Ahmed translated this to Naji who took Charles' hand uttering a torrent of Arabic.

'He says you are a true friend now,' said Ahmed. 'He says he will give his head for yours.' (Little did he know then how close we would come to it.)

We drove to a nearby house standing alone on the outskirts of old Marib. Out of it stepped Saleh Al Saqqaf, a man in his late sixties, dressed in a white turban and long coat. He was to lead our little expedition. He invited us inside. Stepping into the darkened recesses of the room, I glimpsed a female figure in the corner. Her waist-length curly black hair almost hid her face. It was Saleh's daughter. Enveloped in a blue dress, she was highlighted against the pale mud wall, like a figure from a Mughal miniature. Saleh Al Saqqaf put his hand on his *jambia*, picked up his Kalashnikov from the floor and said, '*yallah*! Let's go.'

The road to Sirwah, passes through great lava fields, the rocks piled high like slag heaps and oxidised deep red. Then come the flattened Guilin-like hills, breaking the monotony of the surrounding wasteland.

A convoy of four-wheel-drive vehicles came towards us. Naji and Ahmed sat up alert and watched carefully as they drove by. Few people had plunged so deep into this part of the interior recently. In fact, back in Sana'a, Marco had suggested we might be the first professional photographers to visit the site.

'There is our baby,' said Ahmed pointing his cigarette towards a cluster of buildings ahead.

We drove into Sirwah past a set of one storey houses with blue shutters. A man with an orange turban waved us through.

The road ended abruptly about five hundred metres from the ancient fortress of Sirwah and we took out our camera equipment.

Charles had set up the tripod, and just mounted the Hasselblad on to it when a precocious young boy of about eleven approached us. It was obvious from the outset that he was going to make trouble.

'No, no, no,' he shouted swinging his index finger like a metronome. He stood directly in front of the camera.

'You are not a respectful person,' Naji shouted at him. Upset by this, the boy moved over to Naji and started shouting again. A crowd of noisy children quickly gathered. A boy touting coral and silver jewellery, rushed in front trying to sell his wares.

Then a teenager came running from a distance, with a *jambia*.

'No, no, no,' once again he screamed, rushing at the tripod as if he was going to push it over. He then pulled his ragged jacket over his head and pointed to me. I went back to the vehicle and sat inside. Then worse was to follow. The teenager opened the Toyota door and tried to pull me out. He did this repeatedly while Naji argued with the others.

'Why can't they take a photo in peace?' yelled Ahmed. 'What a way to treat guests to our country, who have come across the world to see Yemen. How would you feel if you went across the world and they did the same to you?'

To offend against a vulnerable person is disgraceful in tribal life and the act must be repudiated by other tribesmen around who are witnesses. The way these boys were behaving was as much an insult to Ahmed and Naji, as it was to us.

'We told you never to come here again,' one of the older boys said to Saleh Al Saqqaf, our guide. This was very bad news and I felt an ache in my stomach. They were contemptuous of all outsiders.

Naji argued with them for ten minutes, their shouts becoming louder and louder. Visible threats were being made; the young men, egged on by each other, glared at us. Naji started shouting *ayb*, (shame on you!) an expression often used if someone mistreats a guest or travelling companion. Charles took down the tripod, packed the camera away and we left before a catastrophe occurred. This was no place to linger. We made a dash for it, driving at breakneck speed out of the village – the man with the orange turban, who had waved us in, now had a gun trained on us. Naji was shouting, 'Let them eat stones!' out of the window, his nerves stretched taut. I kept a watchful eye out behind us in case anyone followed. Above us were gun emplacements dug into the hilltops. Even the army had been deployed and were camped outside the town to sort out the problems of the tribes that lived here. After about ten minutes we knew we were clear, and stopped. I felt we were totally incompetent to cope with anything at this point. Ahmed left the vehicle carrying Saleh Al Saqqaf's Kalashnikov. Charles followed him and they walked to the back of the Toyota. They strutted about like large birds released from a pen to relieve stress. I could see how easy it was to get angry in this part of the world, and thought that Ahmed might even fire the gun into the air – as a traditional way of warning intruders to stay away.

The area was well-known for kidnapping and territorial rights were zealously fought over. It is not uncommon in some parts of Yemen to take a hostage to advertise a grievance. Most commonly it is to alert the government to the need for an electricity supply, new roads, or else schools or hospitals. Sometimes it is for money, or to obtain a free four-wheel-drive. A Palestinian Jordanian friend once told me that 'Camels may be the ships of the desert... but the Bedu are the pirates!'

Certainly the young villagers of Sirwah were very wary of strangers, and it was probably the hard struggle of life that made them like this. Moreover Saleh hadn't warned us that he had already had a disagreement with them. We had no business being there as far as they were concerned. We realised why no one, not even Yemenis went there.

It was lunch by the time we arrived back in Marib from this unsettling experience, and we ate and rested while the sun moved across the sky. At about four o'clock Naji drove us to the edge of the old city where we picked our way across the dried-up channels and gravel banks of the Wadi Adhana outwash plain. The incense traders had long gone. The rise of Christianity, which did not use incense to the same extent, the fall of the Roman Empire and the discovery of sea routes to India all in their turn contributed to its demise. But beneath our feet lay their once treasured possessions – potsherds, fragments of marble, alabaster and glass beads scattered over the ground in abundance like a midden. I could hear them crunch beneath my feet.

A few houses were still occupied in the old city, itself built on centuries of other buildings to form a great mound, which could be seen from miles around. The first building we entered had a large hall-way recently constructed using old Sabaean columns to support the roof. It was a temporary mosque and the warm late afternoon wind blew through the empty space to offer some relief from the searing heat. Climbing up into the village, half covered with desert sand, it resembled an archeological dig. We stumbled over fallen walls and wound our way through a few narrow alleyways. Many of the build-ings were very tall and had crumbled. Missing walls exposed the floors and staircases inside. It felt like early 1960s Swansea, where bombed-out buildings on street corners doubled as adventure playgrounds. In a place that once had over one hundred fine buildings, now perhaps only twenty or thirty people lived. It was the type of site that propels the imagination into over-drive, in the effort to piece back the miss-ing walls and doors. It was hard to believe that this was once the capital of the Sabaeans, probably the greatest of the ancient kingdoms of Yemen, whose inscriptions proclaimed their presence from the eighth century BC to about 275 AD.

I heard a female voice calling. Above me, leaning out of a window in a mud wall, a woman was gesturing to a neighbour below. Her head-scarf was full of green and blue threads cascading around her head. Her jewellery caught the orange light of the sun and flickered like fire. Turning a corner, I saw what appeared to have been a modern building, now rubble on the ground. A passer-by stopped and spoke to Ahmed.

'This was a building, only just finished when the earthquake in 1982 brought it crashing to the ground, he says,' explained Ahmed. 'But look at these old mud buildings, they were made from ingredients which included eggs – many of them survived the quake. But they are old now and people have moved into modern Marib down the road.'

We left Marib to drive on a few kilometres to some archaeological sites, the four-wheel drive bobbing left and right to avoid the soft sand. *Awwam*, the great temple of Marib – sometimes called Mahram Bilqis, (*mahram* means 'place of refuge') is dedicated to the moon god Almaqah and was partly excavated by Wendell Phillips of the American Expedition in 1952. It is by far the largest temple complex in Southern Arabia and one of the earliest. Though largely unexcavated, the site holds the key to finally establishing the existence of the Queen of Sheba as a definite historical figure like the Queens of ancient Egypt, Hatshepsut and Cleopatra, who already have proven identities.

We moved on to a row of eight monolithic pillars, probably a propylon – a gateway marking the entrance to the temple. It was a reminder that kingdoms rise and fall.

Nearby stood the Arsh Bilqis (the Throne of Bilqis), also known as the Almaqah or Moon Temple. It was the second most important building in Marib, with its line of five elegant symmetrical pillars. The pure abstraction and geometrisation can be seen in Yemeni structures even today.

Yet it was the Marib Dam, the construction of which began in the early sixth century BC, that is the real treasure of the area. Situated seven kilometres southwest of the city, it is one of the world's great ancient structures. Its purpose was to collect water during the rainy season in Wadi Adhana for subsequent irrigation. The *wadi* is the largest in the South Arabian highlands, and the drive alongside it spectacular. It is a sun-bleached wilderness of dry crevasses. The dam is a witness to the highly organised society that built and maintained it. Highly advanced systems were developed to collect and store water, cisterns, aqueducts, irrigation dams, even the terraced fields themselves.

Cameras in hand we walked up to the northern sluice-gate. I focused on some details on the wall, admiring the finely dressed stone. The mastering of the techniques to quarry, cut, finish and carry the stones to site and then erect and bind them together with lead and iron, was impressive. The Sabaeans were expert builders, their masons cutting blocks so finely that they worked usually without mortar. Walking further up on to a rocky outcrop I could focus on the southern sluice gate across the *wadi*. The structure here is more extensive and almost reaches its original height.

I had to imagine what the dam was once like. Originally there would have been a six hundred metre-long earth bank between the two sluices, with a rip-rap protection of loose stones. The whole edifice irrigated over 25,000 acres and supported between 25,000 and 50,000 Sabaeans, not to mention the caravaneers and their camels, who may have stocked up on water to see them across the desert.

The dam broke on a number of occasions mainly due to overtop-ping of the earth bank by floodwater, one of the last being in 542 AD during the reign of Abraha the Axumite, the Christian overlord of Ethiopia, a latter day Hannibal who once over-optimistically attempted to take the city of Mecca using elephants. He was famous for his attempts at plugging the dam, which broke for the last time in 570 AD, the birthdate of the Prophet Mohammed. It is said to have engulfed 20,000 men, 14,000 camels and 12,000 pairs of donkeys.

The remaining families migrated north and east after this as far afield as Syria. In 1986 a new dam was opened further upstream, a gift from Sheikh Zayid bin Sultan (Al Nahayan) President of The United Arab Emirates, who believed himself to be a descendant of the tribes that moved north. The new dam collects water from the Al Balak mountain range and is estimated to hold 400 million cubic metres.

Before I first visited Arabia, I had imagined the desert to be a pale beige colour, with flecks of shadow deepened with black. I thought sand dunes resembled the waves of the sea, light and shadow compet-ing for attention. In fact vast areas are full of colour. In Marib it was a dark pink, a result of the iron content, oxidising in the humidity – to a painter a dab of cadmium red and yellow mixed into a bed of white. In my mind I had always thought the desert deep in sand, but there are vast areas of hard gravel plains.

The next day we left Marib at about 4.30am on a tarmac road, guided by Abdul Karim who travelled in a separate vehicle. After about thirty minutes we stopped and Naji let the tyres down to twenty pounds per square inch – so the vehicles could get more grip on the shifting sands.

We moved off road, near some mud houses, and travelled for about two hours before the sun rose. The painter Turner would have been impressed. Dawn, only to be surpassed by the faint outline of a Bedouin encampment in the distance. A family known to Abdul Karim was camped with a few ageing camels in three substantial cotton tents.

An elderly man bearing a long grey Old Testament beard with a remarkably weathered and toothless face welcomed us and invited us for breakfast (hospitality is extremely important in Yemen and not to accept it can be an insult to some people). The old man's khaki coloured gown billowed as he walked, his hand resting on his *jambia*. A few of his male relatives came up to shake our hands, followed by three sisters, their jet black crinkled hair was cut like Cleopatra's with fringes that just touched the edge of their alabaster coloured skin. They looked identical. Even more curious was the swirl of their exotic, brightly-coloured dresses. Their bright, kohl-painted eyes were typical of the Bedu in this region. It was a chance moment of intimacy, of two very different cultures. We were invited to sit down and rest on a long woven green carpet. The boys rushed off and brought us tea and bread. Cool fresh frothy camel's milk was passed around in a bowl.

I was fascinated by the girl's foreheads. They were tattooed with a tree of life pattern, that resembled an ancient candle stick. In pre-Islamic Arabia, animism was prevalent and trees and springs were worshipped. Today this family were camped by a well-head (known in the oil industry as a Christmas tree) they had been paid by a company to stand guard over.

The old man spoke in the purest rhythmic Arabic.

'Where are you from?' he asked, passing a string of *masbahah* (prayer beads) through his fingers. Ahmed translated.

'From Britannia.' said Charles.

'What do you do?'

'We take photographs.'

'How many children do you have?'

'We have none.'

'Why?'

'God has not given us any.'

An owl hooted nearby. Abdul Karim started muttering to himself.

'What is the matter with Abdul Karim?' I asked.

'He hates that owl,' said Ahmed. 'It has tried to attack him in the past – the owl has not been around for two months but came back last week. He's fed up with it.' Abdul Karim was in its territory but also deeply concerned by what I had just said. Some Arabs believe that the owl is the personification of a female demon or *jinn*, that destroys the creative power of men and makes women barren. That an owl had been watching us from a distance made our Bedouin friend nervous.

The sun rose higher in the sky and the shadows slid away as we drove on. Abdul Karim increased his speed. There was nothing on the horizon, only sand stretching away endlessly. It was a flattened landscape that drew you along the road. The journey took many hours, and for much of it we were quite lost in our own thoughts.

After about six hours travelling we came upon another group of Bedouin in an isolated spot. This time, they were set against the vast and empty landscape, there was no camp visible. It was as if the desert was their private back garden. The ground was covered with bushy yellow flowering shrubs and solitary patches of grass on which their camels, goats and sheep were feeding.

It felt as if we were in the middle of nowhere. The desert gave out only silence. We pulled up beside three young women.

'Where are you from, the north or the south?' asked Naji, wondering if we had passed over the old border between the two Yemens.

'Neither,' came the reply 'We are from here.'

Their response rang of concern that their freedom to wander as tribal peoples might be fettered by central government or the military. Their local genealogical tree probably went back thousands of years. Yemen's ancient influence had decayed well before the coming of Islam, and the centre of power had moved to Mecca. But Yemenis, like all Arabs, had moved with Empires, spreading Islam and Arabic. Who were we to question these Bedu?

We drove on, soon large outcrops of rocks came into view. The reds and yellows of the sand turned into purples and blues, heralding the advent of the Al-Abr mountains and the road to Hadramaut. Here long ago a major river flowed into the interior cutting deep into the bedrock. At the time the climate was wetter; now there is just an occasional flash flood.

We arrived at a military outpost in what seemed to be the middle of nowhere. Naji was not interested in the soldiers questions of where we were heading and why; he was hungry again and asked a guard if there was anywhere we could get meat. 'The Bedu... are absolute slaves of their appetite... gluttons for stewed meat,' wrote T.E. Lawrence in his *Seven Pillars of Wisdom*. The guard put down his gun and reached into a small hut and, taking pity, offered Naji a packet of biscuits.

Manhattan of the Desert: Shibam, Hadramaut

The Manhattan of the Desert

'The road is long that has been travelled only once.'
(Welsh proverb)

As soon as we reached the first tarmac road we stopped for a hearty meal of lamb and rice. It was not long before Ahmed and Naji had also found a large bundle of qat. The late afternoon light in the Hadramaut is beautiful, and we jumped back into the Landcruiser for the final part of our journey. Long shadows cast cubist shapes between buildings and enriched their colour. There was an unusual silence too. Every sound travelled uniquely and reached our ears like notes on a musical score. One minute it was the bleat of a sheep, the next the stuttering of a motorcycle.

Your first impressions of Shibam are never forgotten. Nothing can prepare you for the spectacle, whether you have seen aerial photographs of the town or an artist's impression of it, covered in honeyed light at sunrise or sunset. The mud skyscrapers form an uninterrupted rampart, rising sheer from the valley floor.

It was late afternoon as we approached and the vast mud city served as a backdrop to a group of boys playing football on a pitch of dried clay, which, after floods, form part of a moat around Shibam.

Perhaps nowhere in Yemen more than here, does the traveller reflect on the masterful skills of the local builders.

Shibam has over five-hundred mud-brick houses, several centuries old, rising to seven or eight storeys. The tallest reaches thirty metres, and is the reason that Freya Stark called it 'The Manhattan of the Desert.' It was added to UNESCO's World Heritage list in 1982. The city's height is exaggerated by the abundance of windows – usually open with wooden shutters, or harem grilles, and ventilation open-ings; often two at different levels on each floor. The lines created by corners and edges of individual buildings adds to this heightening effect, as do the long dark shadows created by the afternoon sun.

Shibam has been the commercial and political capital of Hadramaut many times in its history and was situated on an impor-tant incense and spice route that brought it wealth and fame. Although the origins of the city are not fully known, it was trading at the time of the Sabaeans in the 4th–5th centuries BC. The first settlement here was built around the 3rd century AD, after the destruction of Shabwa, Yemen's foremost ancient city, now just an archaeological site.

Ahmed had many times described the flavour of Hadrami tea and led us to a small tea house on the outer edge of the city. We sat on a raised balcony, overlooking a cluster of palm groves, the shadows of their fronds making patterns on the ground. Women shrouded in black crossed the open ground beneath us. A few camels roamed. The silence was broken only by the occasional vehicle.

Finishing our tea we continued through the gates of Shibam. Goats guarded the entrance, children played hopscotch and the sound of a *mizmar* (a pipe with double reeds) competed with a crowing cockerel. A cat darted across our path as we walked by a group of older men sitting cross-legged playing dominoes.

We walked on through the narrow streets setting up our tripods, catching movements of people in their daily lives, trying to make the photographs breathe. Many of the rich sandy-coloured mud buildings were in different stages of repair and renovation. Carefully placed wooden shutters were painted grey, green and soft pink. It was a minimalist dream of subtle decoration on vast planes of wall space.

The following year I was to return to Shibam when it was full of wedding parties and a procession of musicians walked through the main square. I slept in a house on the outskirts of the town wall. One morning I woke to hear children singing, the sound and rhythm of their voices reminded me of music I had heard in Java in the late 1980s. It was as if the children had learnt traditional sailing songs brought back by local men on ships.

Only fifty years before this area was bedevilled by feuding and internecine conflict between families and tribes.

We headed on before sunset to Seiyun, capital of Wadi Hadramaut, which is about half an hour's drive east of Shibam. We passed mud villages nestling among the valley's myriad palm groves. Women swathed in black, wearing tall conical straw hats (*madhalla*) sifted earth for bricks, or were herding sheep and goats, hauntingly stirring up the dust, or working in fields green with lucerne and other crops; we could hear the throb of diesel pumps irrigating farms and date gardens in the cool of the evening. According to Hassan Ali Ba Humaid, the local director of tourism, several million palm trees grow in Wadi Hadramaut and its tributary valleys.

Seiyun's history stretches back into antiquity, but a turning point came in 1494 AD with an influx of people from the Hamdani tribes north of Sana'a. Their leader, Badr Bu Tuwairiq Al-Kathiri, was the ancestor of the Kathiri Sultans who ruled a gradually shrinking area of Hadramaut from 1516 until the British left South Arabia in 1967.

Later that evening we sat out on the patio of our hotel under an almost full moon amid clusters of stars as brilliant as sequins against the black velvet of the night sky. The natural light was so strong that it cast shadows around where we sat and lit the lime-washed walls and parapets of even distant buildings, and brought the cliff walls of the escarpment on either side of the valley into clear relief. Watching this timeless scene in the dry desert air stirred our thoughts. Perhaps a night sky of comparable brilliance inspired Yemen's Rasulid King, Al-Ashraf 'Umar bin Yusuf, to write his treatise on the astrolabe – the instrument used to calculate the movement of celestial bodies and Muslim prayer times.

The following morning we visited the palace of the former Kathiri Sultan which today houses a museum of archaeology and folklore, including displays of local costumes and artifacts, and a library of historical documents. It is the single largest mud-brick building in Hadramaut, with its massive walls and soaring turrets plastered and painted a dazzling white. We explained our photographic project to an elderly attendant who had once worked for a British couple living in Seiyun before independence. He guided us amiably through the palace's labyrinth of rooms. It was a relief to feel cool air blowing

through the carved lattice windows. Their distinctive keyhole apertures resembled a chess game, crowns of kings and queens, the strong
forms of castles and knights, even pawns silhouetted against the
bright sun. We could see the traffic in the street below weaving
through crowds of pedestrians. Here, no Kalashnikovs were to be
seen. The town had an atmosphere of good order and civic spirit, and
its streets seemed generally free of the piles of rubbish which litter so
many urban centres in highland Yemen.

Tarim is the last of the three important towns in Wadi Hadramaut.
Overshadowed by vast rock cliffs on one side and surrounded by palm
groves on the other, it has been the religious capital of the region since
the tenth century, and scholars from across the Islamic world, especially South East Asia, continue to study at its famous religious
academy, al-Ribat, which was established in 1886. But Tarim is also
renowned for its numerous mud-brick palaces built between the two
World Wars by Hadrami families who had made fortunes trading in
the Far East, notably Singapore and Java. The architecture of these
palaces is strikingly eclectic. The craftsmen who built here seem to
have created an architectural encyclopaedia in mud reflecting British
and Dutch colonial as well as Indo-Saracenic influences. For example,
the 'Ishshah Palace combines a facade of Corinthian columns with
Mughal-style windows. Another palace is pure Art Deco, while yet
another, Munaysurah, is essentially neo-classical. Even in their dere-
liction today, they all testify to the wealth and power of the merchant
princes who returned to their homeland to have them built. Such
people also built and endowed mosques all over Tarim – so many, in
fact, that it used to be said that one could pray in a different mosque
every day of the year. The most impressive of these is the Al-Mihdhar
Mosque which was built in 1915 and, unusually, has a square minaret.

We also wanted to see the famous Al-Ahqaf Library in Tarim. We
walked up a flight of steps adjacent to a mosque and found ourselves
in a room lined with glass-fronted cupboards crammed with books.
Sheikh Ali Salem Bukair, the curator, librarian and manuscript artist
came over to welcome us. He asked us whether we knew Professor
Robert Serjeant who had devoted much of his academic life to the
study of the language, society and history of Hadramaut. We replied

no, not personally, but we knew of his work.

The library houses around 5,000 manuscripts, many ancient, collected from the surrounding region, relating to religion, the thoughts of the prophet, Islamic law, sufism, medicine, astronomy, agriculture, biography, history and mathematics. Many are illuminated or illustrated with vibrant drawings. Ali Salem opened the cupboard and brought one out.

'It is old,' he said.

'How old?' I asked.

'Five hundred years.'

Taking Sheikh Ali at his word, I thought back. 1492 exactly, the fall of the Kingdom of Granada and the end of Muslim rule in Spain. He gently placed the book on a nearby table so that we could photograph it. The book showed the Kaaba in Mecca and the surrounding regions of the Islamic world, shaped into a circle like the earth.

Over fifteen hundred years earlier Eratosthenes (275-194 BC), the third librarian of Alexandria had seen the masts of ships slowly revealing themselves above the horizon. He was an early sceptic. He calculated the differing shadow lengths at noon between Aswan and Alexandria and thought that the world could not be flat. By 1492, the date of this illumination, in the sheltered archives of Tarim, a further fifty years was to pass before Nicolas Copernicus published 'On the Revolutions of Heavenly spheres' (1543) which challenged by mathematics rather than observational astronomy the ancient teaching that the sun revolved around the earth. The earth revolves around the sun. Seeing is not always believing.

Little Ben and the R.C. Church, Aden

The Coal-Hole of the East

'God so loved this country he left it as it was'
(Yemeni saying)

'Spanish, Dutch not so good. Allemani, Fransi, and Itali good people,' said Naji. 'Americans OK too, but sit like this,' he sat bolt upright. We were driving down from the Hadramaut to Aden and it was going to be a long journey. We were to cross over the great Jaul, a semi-desert mountain plateau north of the port of Mukalla, where we planned to stop over.

The villages on the road out of the Hadramaut were impressive, built of dried mud-brick anchored deep into the bedrock of the valley sides, often painted with lime-wash and highly decorated with bright pink, blues, greens and yellows. As we drove by Wadi Doan, Ahmed asked Naji to stop.

'Stop, stop you are always telling me to stop! We have to get to Mukalla!'

'But I want to get some honey!' Ahmed shouted back.

'Well why didn't you say you needed medicine!' Naji retorted.

Honey is probably the most important medication in Islam.

Ahmed looked back at us.

'You want some honey?'

We said we would love some.

'Wait here a minute. I will check if it's pure and no one has added sugar to it.'

Ahmed wandered off. Just as Naji checked meat, Ahmed was checking the honey.

Hadramaut's strong-flavoured honey is the most expensive honey in the world and the most expensive food you can buy in Yemen. Its unique taste and quality is due to colonies of bees feeding on desert bushes and the blossom of the *'ilb* and *sidr* trees, *Zizyphus spina-Christi* (Christ's thorn). Many Yemeni beekeepers are semi-nomadic and move to different areas when the flowers are in season.

Yemen's rock engravings reveal that beekeeping is one of the oldest forms of food-gathering in the region, and at one time practically every house in the vast area of the Wadi Doan had a hive. Honey was so precious a commodity that the Prophet Mohammed forbade the killing of honey bees. Al-Hamdani, the tenth-century geographer, noted that some honey in Yemen was so thick it had to be cut with a knife. It is widely believed to have aphrodisiac in addition to therapeutic qualities. Every traveller should appreciate the worth of the honeybee. I recall being told by my primary school headmaster that Ulysses put beeswax into the ears of his sailors to protect them from the voices of the Sirens at sea. For Mr Evans the *Iliad* and the *Odyssey* competed with the Old Testament at lessons each day in Assembly. He was a classicist from Aberdare, the home of Welsh scholars and real travellers – those who travelled with their imagination. Mr Evans covered all the corridors of our school in Cardiff with subtle prints of *The Arabian Nights* and taught us the importance of mythologies. John Albert Evans, then our Welsh language teacher, admitted that he loved the school so much he hated taking holidays. But why would you need holidays when every morning Mr Evans took you on a journey?

Ahmed returned.

'Yes it is good honey, come and see.'

We walked up a dusty path and into a small roadside shop. In front of us, on a wooden table, stood rows of shiny tins of the kind which we had seen being made out of recycled oil drums in Seiyun's market. Oil and honey. The man behind the counter opened a few for us – inside was the honeycomb – glistening and dripping. We negotiated a price, and to Naji's relief we continued at speed towards Mukalla, passing more hives on our way. We stopped at the village of Ras Howra for lamb cooked by local Bedouin. Fried in sesame oil pressed using a camel in a nearby building, and coated with spices, it surpassed any other meal we were to eat in the whole country.

Our journey continued across the Jaul, great dry land formations petering out into a huge desert to the north. It was near here, we learned later that a burial ground of mummified camels each placed in a large sarcophagus of their own, had just been discovered. This was a region for ancient caravan routes, yet a place still too remote until recently for archaeological attention.

Our first sight of Mukalla was the top of the tall Rawdah minaret in the suburb which stretched out around the bay of Khalf. The traveller Hans Helfritz, wrote in the 1930s 'Mukalla, a city of glistening whiteness, of extraordinary beauty, with its countless palaces and lofty towers, lies in a delightful bay close under the dark cliffs of the Jebel el Kara. It is the gateway to the province of Hadramaut.'

The two main historic ports here are Mukalla itself and nearby Shihr, which are famous for their fishing fleets. Marco Polo, in his travels in the thirteenth century, wrote about Shihr on the coast as one of the most barren places in the world. He described it as a huge city with a good harbour, where heavily-laden ships from India docked. Renowned for the quality of its incense, ships sailed from here carrying vast numbers of Arabian horses, chargers and saddle horses to India where they were sold at great profit.

Mukalla is the second most important port in southern Yemen after Aden, and in 1914 supplanted Shihr as the capital of the Quaiti Sultanate. Its waterfront activity is still paramount despite new roads; in the past most people would have approached Mukalla by sea. In the nearby narrow streets, intricate Mogul-like doors welcome you at the entrances of run-down buildings.

When we arrived the main square was bustling with street traders, workers and fishermen playing cards and dominoes in the tea houses. We joined them and watched the sun sink, immersing the lime-washed buildings in luminous pink light. The fairy lights adorning the minaret were switched on and the muezzin called out his summons to prayer.

The Sultan's palace at Mukalla, decorated with Indian and neoclassical influences, sits on seafront and is now a museum. The next day we travelled west from Mukalla towards Aden along a fringe of pure white sand, cut in two by the coastal road, and occasionally interrupted by sprawling volcanic rocks. The mounds of ghost crab provided sporadic decorations on the beach where turtles come ashore to lay their eggs. Isolated fishermen's huts stood on spits of sand. We crossed the bridge spanning the Wadi Hajar, one of Yemen's few perennial rivers, and drove for hours until our first natural break at Bir Ali. After eating shark and rice in a local restaurant, Ahmed and Naji, exhausted, fell asleep. Charles and I took out our cameras beneath Husn al Ghurab, an extinct volcano undercut by surf which guards the entrance to a port famous in antiquity.

The beach was of pure white sand and the sea lay flat, clear blue-green and eerily silent. The sky looked like an empty canvas, with a soft wash, waiting for an artist. Craggy black-grey fields of basaltic lava extended down into the water resembling mounds of washed coal.

On the landward north side, we walked around the base of the volcano. Basalt blocks laid out like the base structures of any archae-ological site, mark all that remains of the streets and houses of this ancient town. The bulk of the material was cannibalised and reused in the buildings of the modern Bir Ali on the other side of the bay.

The bay of Bir Ali, or Qana as it was once called, was the main port of the Kingdom of Hadramaut until the end of the second century AD. Into it came precious goods, mainly diamonds, cotton and lapis lazuli from India, gold and ivory from East Africa, and frankincense from Dhofar and Somalia. It is mentioned by Pliny, and earlier in the Old Testament book of Ezekiel. 27:23. Goods would have been transferred from the ships in the harbour to small rafts and boats bringing them ashore to the waiting caravans. Camels would then make the 60-70 day journey via Shabwa, to Mecca in Saudi Arabia, and then to Petra in Jordan, or to Gaza which at one point during the first millennium BC was ruled over by King Solomon.

Bir Ali felt a special place, offering space for the imagination. Our next town was Azzan, from where locals say one of the magi follow-ing the star that visited Christ was born.

'Please stop Naji, this architecture is wonderful. Look at the height of the mud buildings. The palm trees... that group of houses,' said Charles. But he was upset by the telegraph poles and wires that clut-tered the buildings.

'Charles is upset by the wires,' said Ahmed, turning to Naji laughing.

'What, the wires! We have only had electricity – ten years!' replied Naji. 'Go, buy a scissors Charles, and I will cut the ones you don't like for your photo!'

Our next stop was Habban, on the edge of the Wadi Habban, set among tall green trees built low on the banks of Wadi Habban and framed on all sides by majestic table mountains. It was once noted for its Jewish silversmiths. The light was beginning to fade but Naji and Ahmed had only just bought qat to chew. As the qat set in so their spirits rose and songs were sung as we crossed the ash-coloured Lawder plain, passing termite mounds and men praying.

'The qat is giving us concentration and energy', said Ahmed.

'Do the Yemeni football team chew it then?' asked Charles.

'No, but it may be a good idea if they did,' said Ahmed.

It was late afternoon as we drove into Aden. We had left the wide, open expanses of landscape behind us, for the confinement of the port's looming volcanic mountains. It was here that Yemenis believe Noah chose to build his great vessel, the ark. Life in the south of the country revolves around the ocean. The port was once one of the richest, busiest and best natural harbours in the world.

I took out the 1960s 'Welcome to Aden' Services handbook I had bought in a second hand bookshop back in Tintern in Wales. Its pages were full of advertisements – 90 years of Luke Thomas, shipping agents, The British Bank of the Middle East, Rover, Aden Airways 'an associate of BOAC', BP international bunkering and Cory Brothers & Company Ltd (Aden Coal Company Ltd) which was started as a shipbroking and coal exporting business in Cardiff Docks in 1842. Even HP sauce had a full page advertisement: sole agents in Aden – The Elite Stores. Sections on the RAF bus service, No 8 Squadron, Aden Women's Voluntary Services, Khormaksar Sailing Club and Christ Church were all there. Most interesting for us at that moment was a photograph of the Crescent Hotel, advertising 'All bedrooms with private baths or showers, all bedrooms air conditioned, a roof garden and restaurant à la carte.'

'I've not been back to Aden for over 20 years' said Ahmed as we turned a corner into the forecourt of the Crescent Hotel. 'God so loved this country he left it as it was.'

Once a busy social centre for the expatriate and British population, it now lay run-down and almost deserted, lost in time like the rest of Aden.

'Perhaps they loved the British so much they left it as it was!' I responded 'or perhaps they were just too lazy to change it. Let's see if they have rooms for the night.'

We walked towards the reception area, leaving Naji pondering over the engine of the Landcruiser.

A 1950s English breakfast menu still hung on the wall. I glanced past it into the empty dining room, cheered only by the sight of a framed David Shepherd print on the wall. There was a layer of dust everywhere, and a broken lift sat trapped inside its metal cage. Ahmed tapped his fingers on the wooden reception desk.

'Do you have rooms for us tonight?' asked Ahmed.

'Of course, we always have rooms,' came the perfunctory reply from the man sitting behind the desk.

'Ask if we can have the room Queen Elizabeth is said to have stayed in during her visit here in 1954,' I said to Ahmed.

'Oh no sorry a Danish man is in that room already, he was waiting two weeks for it,' said the man sitting up in his seat. 'But there are plenty of other rooms.'

We followed the receptionist up the stairs and along a bare, poorly-lit corridor. He came to a halt and held out a key.

The door was flung open to emit the stale odours of human occupation.

'The bed is filthy,' I said. I wandered into the en suite bathroom. The bathroom had not been cleaned for months. There was a large window at one end overlooking the street below, and there was not even a net curtain.

The receptionist was still hovering outside the door. I suggested to Ahmed he ask the man to get the room cleaned.

'He says they have no staff to do it,' replied Ahmed, watching me unravel the dirty sheets.

'Well does he have some cleaning fluid then?'

'No, he says he doesn't have such a thing. But he can find clean sheets, and there is a shop on the corner of the street that sells cleaning fluid.'

The receptionist said a few brief words, turned his back and left.

'Ahmed and I will go down to the main road and get some cleaning fluid.' said Charles.

On his return, Charles said 'You'll never believe this Pat, but the man in the shop recognised Ahmed after twenty years.'

Ahmed was nodding his head.

'I am home,' he said.

I then took myself into the bathroom to do the cleaning. The taps spat out water intermittently, with a sound reminiscent of a dying animal. I scrubbed every centimetre of the place, then looked out into the night sky. The former British Colony was quiet, but I felt an unease. I decided that I couldn't face a night's sleep there. Despite its age and history, the Crescent Hotel had seen better days.

'Ahmed says there is another hotel in town – the Aden Mövenpick Hotel, but it is the most expensive hotel in Yemen.'

We collected all our things and left the Crescent without billing them for our cleaning services. The attitude of the staff was found wanting, like our experience of Soviet Russia a few years previously: everyone sitting around waiting for someone else to do the work.

The Sales Manager of the Mövenpick, Aidroos Obeid approached us after breakfast.

'I hear you are looking for old British links,' he said excitedly.

'Yes, do you know of any?' I replied.

'Oh there are many. So many people remember the old days of the British here. I left this place when the communists were here and went to Saudi Arabia and the Gulf. The period after the British left was a disaster for us here. Nothing happened, everything closed down. I'll introduce you to the hotel manager.'

We were shuffled into a side room. A man rose to shake our hands.

'You are from Cardiff, I understand.'

'That's right,' replied Charles.

'Well, well.' He slid a letter across the desk.

I read the address on the top. 'This says 142 Bute Street, Cardiff!'

I was astonished.

'Yes I have a relative living there. We all know about Cardiff, it is famous here. Many of us have relatives in Britain. I'm from Sheffield,' he said rather proudly.

We explained our project to do research for a television programme and a book. We discussed the history of Aden, the coal bunkering, and the Cardiff-Aden connections.

'You must go down to Ma'alla where the Aden Bunkering Company is located, they can give you some more information.' he said.

I arranged to meet Charles downstairs and went to get Ahmed. While we were in the lift descending to the lobby we met a young Welsh mud logging contractor working for Canadian Occidental. Ahmed looked at me with the kind of resignation you need on these journeys. It was 9.00am and the day was already blessed.

The Aden Bunkering Company was housed in a long, low-lying building sitting comfortably on the edge of the sea. Charles and I left Ahmed and Naji in the vehicle outside and wandered in and around the courtyard. Behind us lay the modern harbour, dotted with a few old Arab *dhows*, and fishermen up to their waists in water, casting nets.

I nearly tripped over some old discarded chains half submerged in the harbour water. They looked familiar, almost certainly manufactured at Brown Lenox in Pontypridd, South Wales. At eighteen I had photographed all over the old workshops. All the early forging tools still hung on the walls. The company was originally the Newbridge Chain Cable and Anchor Works, founded in 1806, using Rhondda coal and Merthyr iron. In their day the greatest chain makers in the world, and the first company to receive Lloyd's approval for ship use. The company became world-renowned as designers and manufacturers of mooring chains, bell moorings and beacon buoys used in the ports of the Empire, including Aden. With clients like Isambard Kingdom Brunel, they supplied all the chain for the *Great Eastern* as well as large Admiralty anchors for many of the worlds greatest ships. From 1808-1916 they had the annual contract to supply the Royal Navy. My father worked there before and during the Second World War, as well as on special projects for them over a span of fifty years. He is obsessed by ships' anchors and did his Masters degree at

Imperial College, London, on their history and design. As a child I spent hours with him on Gower beaches pulling anchors through the sand and thinking of far-off places.

Charles and I wandered back towards the main door and offices. Everything here seemed so familiar, something about the place smelt of my childhood, and it was reassuring. 1950s and 60s British architecture, signwriting and a sense of order were all there.

I spoke to a typist in the office.

'We are looking to find out about where the coal used to be brought ashore and bunkered.'

'Well I'll have to go and ask the manager and see if he can help you.'

We waited for a few minutes and she returned.

'Come with me.'

We were taken through into a large room with plans all around the walls. A rotund, cheerful man rose from behind a desk to shake our hands.

'How can I help you?'

'We are looking to find out something about the history of the coal coming to Aden from Britain, particularly from Wales.'

'Sit, sit down please,' he said gesturing to us.

He smiled, then I mentioned that my father had once been a mine surveyor in the coal pits of the Welsh Valleys. That my great grandfather had been a coal leveller, making sure that ships were safe to leave port with coal and that many of the ships he had prepared came to Aden.

Turning to his desk drawer, he opened it and brought out about eight pieces of coal, and threw them across the surface of the desk, like dice.

'This is what you are looking for is it?' he said laughing.

Charles and I looked at each other, then at the pieces of coal. It was like stumbling across a cache of buried treasure.

I said 'I can't believe you keep them in your drawer! These are Welsh, I think'.

A look of amazement spread across the manager's face. What was the appeal of something so ordinary?

'This is steam coal, the very best,' I said, holding a piece in my hand. 'You can sometimes tell by the shape, and its inherent strength. It doesn't crumble easily.'

He sat back in his chair, amused. No coal had been bunkered here for nearly half a century.

'Well we keep digging to repair pipes around here and all we find is coal in the ground. It's everywhere!'

This was the Aden described by the nineteenth century explorer Richard Burton as 'the coal-hole of the East'

'What can we do to find out more?' I asked.

'Well you can start just over there,' he said pointing out of the window. 'Ali Salam Fawz is building a house across the road and all he finds on his plot of land is coal. Go along the road a bit until you see an old black Ford car. That's his. I'm sure he would be very interested to meet you.'

We thanked him, left the room and went back on to the main road. Ahmed and Naji were deep in conversation.

'You won't believe this' I said. I held out a brown envelope and dropped the coal the manager had given us on to my palm.

'My God! Where did you get that from?' exclaimed Ahmed sitting up in his seat.

'From the manager. It's unbelievable, he was keeping it in his drawer!' said Charles.

'We have to go down the road here. There is a man building a house, he apparently has coal in his basement.' I said.

Naji, who inspected the coal with his fingers, straightened up and with new vigour moved the Landcruiser forward down the road as I pointed to a polished old black Ford, parked outside a compound wall. Naji laughed, he couldn't believe that there was such an old car still on the road.

Ahmed led us through the gate. Before us was a partially finished one storey concrete building standing at the foot of a volcanic outflow. All around us in the courtyard were redundant old Ford cars and spare parts. A young man came out of the building and exchanged greetings with Ahmed, and then with us. Ahmed quickly spoke in Arabic. The young man began to laugh and raise his voice.

'Come, Come.' he beckoned us into the dwelling. Inside a mature woman dressed in a beautiful shade of purple sat on the edge of a bed. Above her a ceiling of wooden beams was partly open to the sky. The walls were newly cemented. Pieces of carpet were thrown across the floor, a hookah and an old pair of British Army binoculars leant against an old earthenware pot.

Ali Salam Fawz, turbaned and smiling came towards us. His hair was dyed red with henna, and he had a smart razor-edged white moustache. His wrinkled sun-burnt skin told of many years in Aden's sun. We were offered tea and sat down.

'He says he knows what you are looking for,' said Ahmed. 'He has just been building this house and in the foundations all he found was coal.'

'Lets go outside.'

Ali Salam Fawz led us outside and walked over to a small wooden shed and opened the door. Dragging a great hessian sack across the yard floor he said.

'Look, Look.' He put his hands deep into the sack and pulled out dusty pieces of coal.

His excitement was palpable.

'He says he is now selling the coal to a local blacksmith.' said Ahmed. 'It must be one hundred years old. The whole house is built on top of a coal bunker.'

'How old is Ali?' I asked Ahmed,

'He says he is 67 years old.'

'Yes, wait a minute.' Ahmed continued talking in Arabic and turned to us. 'He says that when he was about thirteen he worked with the coal. He used to work on the barges that carried the coal off the ships that docked here. It was very hard, carrying bags of coal with your bare hands. They used to throw it on to the bunkers around here. He later worked as a driver for BP, when the coal ended and it was replaced by oil.'

The way to take on board coal varied in different parts of the world. In Britain coal was often lifted hydraulically in wagons and tipped straight into the ship. It was a dirty job my great grandfather was involved in. In Aden and the Far East men often carried coal with their bare hands, on a shovel, or in baskets, on to barges or by running up and down planks from the quay. If they were lucky the coal would be bagged.

Ali pointed above us at a pipe running down the mountain.

'He says this is where they used to get the water from for the steamships.'

'What about Cardiff? Has he heard of it?'

Ahmed turned and continued to speak to him.

'Yes, he says he remembers when he was a boy the men going on to the ships. He would ask them where they were going. 'Cardiff for Coal' they all used to say. But he was too young to go.'

Ali pointed to his Ford Prefect.

'It was built in 1940,' said Ahmed, translating.

'This is his dream car, he doesn't want to forget the old days,' said Ahmed. 'Many people even from the British Embassy have come to him wanting to give him good money for the car, but he refused. It is still in good working order.'

Ali nodded.

'If they take his car he says he will not be in good heart,' said Ahmed, 'it is good luck for him – it is his mascot.'

* * *

The position of Aden near the entrance to the Red Sea, made it a crucial landfall on the ancient trade routes, following the monsoon winds between India and the Mediterranean. With the back door to Egypt a fairly short trip down the Red Sea, the successive influences of Empires – Roman, Byzantine and Ottoman in the region, and Aden's success as a port throughout the major moments in history was without question. During the medieval period it was also an important stopping-off place between India and Africa. Marco Polo wrote about Aden in the fourteenth century saying that; 'I assure you that the Sultan of Aden derives a very large revenue from the heavy duties he levies from the merchants coming and going in his country. Indeed thanks to these, he is one of the richest rulers in the world.'

Many merchants were based in or travelled through Aden, dispatching goods on to Cairo from India and in the opposite direction. Copper, brass, lead and even recycled materials are mentioned in various texts, along with cloves, peppers, raisins and waxes, from Ceylon or Malaysia. There were also silks from China, frankincense from Somalia and Southern Arabia and coffee, saffron and beeswax from northern Yemen. The coffee plantations which had made Yemen famous have now been transplanted into Ceylon, Java, the West Indies and eventually Brazil, sapping the rich trade in the highlands.

In 1893, in *A Journey through Yemen,* W.B. Harris wrote that

> ...Aden perhaps can claim an antiquity and an importance throughout all history unparalleled for its size and its situation, in the annals of the world. When countries, now the centres of vast civilisations consisted of primeval forests, inhabited by almost primeval man, and filled with wild beasts, Aden was an emporium of trade. With every possible disadvantage, except its harbour and its situation, it was inhabited by merchants, who collected and reshipped by vessel and by caravans the wealth of many lands.

Aden suffered a long decline after the Portuguese in the fifteenth and sixteenth centuries found a new route around the Cape of Good Hope. Then in early 1839 the East India Company, with the enforced compliance of the Sultan of Lahej annexed Aden.

The Peninsular and Oriental Steam Company was the first to establish a coal depot at Tawahi (Steamer Point). By 1850 Aden was declared a 'Free Port', (a port where no duties are levied on articles of commerce) and business immediately boomed. The largest trading nation was India. Persian businesses housed here were also set up, yet Captain Luke Thomas was the first to initiate commercial operations. Mail ships, taken over eventually by P&O, had priority status in the harbour, and steamship lines of many nations established depots at Hedjuff. By the 1850s and 60s coal was off-loaded from ships moored offshore by large numbers of workers, many of whom had migrated from the hills of North Yemen, while a further substantial number came from Mocha. Aden's business increased rapidly through British involvement and the building in 1869 of the Suez canal. The arrival of the telegraph in Aden in 1870 gave it an advantage over other Red Sea ports in trade with East Africa, the Far East and Australia. The first temporary accommodation of reed huts around the coaling depots of Tawahi and Ma'alla were later replaced by permanent housing and Yemeni coffee houses filled with people trying to find employment, socialising, eating and collecting wages. Steamships began to arrive in large numbers, replacing sailing ships (partly because of the unreliable winds of the Red Sea) and the port developed. By the end of the century it could handle the largest ships of the day. Yemenis were able to get work on the ships, often as stokers and the bunkering port was one of the world's premier refuelling depots.

Ali Salam Fawz had seen so much change in his life. His Ford car had become a symbol of continuity and stability as well as a reminder of a more prosperous past.

Charles, Ahmed, Naji and myself all went down to the sea to watch the gentle waves breaking. There were brightly coloured fishing boats resting in the water. A few people had gathered to share news. We stared at the quiet horizon in front of us trying to imagine the busy shipping lanes of the past and looked at the wide open spaces where precious mountains of Welsh coal had once sat.

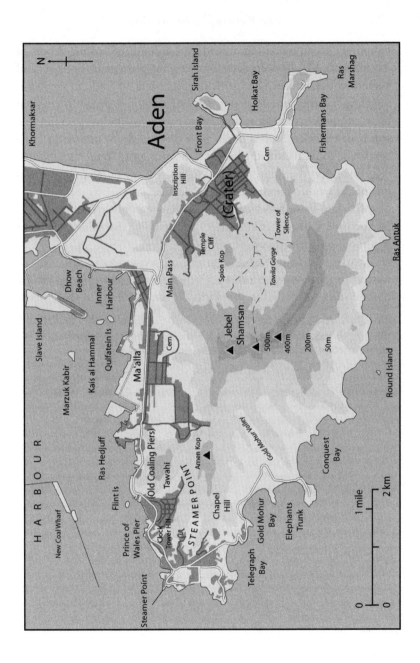

South Wales Borderers' insignia, Aden

The Barren Rocks of Aden

'Oh, East is East and West is West and never the twain shall meet. Till Earth and Sky stand presently at God's great judgement Seat... But there is neither East nor West, Border, nor Breed, nor Birth, When two strong men stand face to face, though they come from the ends of the Earth!' (Rudyard Kipling)

We stopped at the South Wales Borderers' insignia magnificently painted on the side of the cliff face. Here was Main Pass, the secure entrance to Crater, the commercial heart of Aden that sits in an extinct volcano. Why the insignia was kept freshly painted we didn't know – although Aden was the last place the regiment actively served outside the United Kingdom, and the insignia with its sphinx and battle honours so beautifully designed may have been what attracted local attention. Even throughout the communist period it had been kept in good order. One person had said it was the site of a local school bus accident and that British soldiers were the first to arrive on site to attend the wounded and take them to hospital. I could sympathise with that. In South Wales we had had the tragedy of the mining village of Aberfan, being buried by a slag heap. 144 people, including 116 children, died when a school and twenty houses were covered by coal waste. The military helped there too, including a friend of my family who was in the Royal Navy and docked in Cardiff. It was one of the worst disasters of the 1960s, its emotional impact resounding far beyond Wales.

Charles and I took out our cameras, set up the tripod and started to take photographs. A group of young boys were playing football beneath the insignia as trucks and vans sped by. As if from nowhere a man appeared. Probably in his early 40s he struck up a conversation with Ahmed and judging by his behaviour, he was getting annoyed.

Ahmed came over to us.

'I think we had better move on.'

'What's the problem?' I asked.

'They are not used to people taking photographs around here. Everyone is suspicious.'

'Suspicious of what?'

'Well they just don't like people taking photographs full stop, let alone around the harbour, and from up here you have a panoramic view of the harbour and along the coast.'

Certainly the position was a vantage point.

'But we are not photographing over there, we're photographing the insignia.'

'Yes I know,' said Ahmed with surprising patience. 'But people are still recovering from the fact that the country has recently been reunited and there are some who still have sympathy for the Russians who had such an influence here over the past thirty years. This is still a highly sensitive time. Things were controlled here, people didn't have freedom. They just don't understand.'

The man, full of self-importance, and no doubt acting independently just to be a nuisance, stood his ground staring at us. It was a vivid portrait of darker days, when the whole of the south was like a fortress. He was not a man to be trifled with.

'I think we had better stop,' said Charles. 'They'll never understand if we explain what we are trying to do.'

It was a sorry omen. I felt we were being watched. It reminded me of travelling through the ancient sites of Communist China a few years previously. I had ended up in a theatre in Kaifeng, a place at that time rarely visited by westerners. There were a few thousand Chinese sitting with us, yet it was still announced that there were 'foreigners' in the audience.

We packed up our cameras and loaded them into the vehicle. Naji was fed up by our being moved on like this. Fiercely independent, he never liked being told what to do. But few travellers were visiting Aden, and there was still a nervousness in the air, as though people were unsure about the future.

We drove on into Crater, where once disembarked travellers from refuelling ships bought their duty-free goods. As we descended we saw the shanty towns seemingly slipping down the sides of volcanic slopes where Yemenis were eking out an existence. Old colonial buildings sat cheek by jowl with ugly 1970s concrete flats, like packs of cards ready to topple. The state of the buildings was pitiful, with peeling pink and green paint, the result of three decades of decay and inactivity.

'Some things never change,' said Ahmed, reflecting on the streets he had not seen for years. 'My God I remember this place. Down there I used to watch Charlie Chaplin films in the street when I was a child – put on by the British soldiers!'

Naji joined in Ahmed's enthusiasm. It was obvious Ahmed loved Aden with a passion. Naji revealed to us he too had travelled through Aden as a child in the early 1960s, with his father as they left for work in Saudi Arabia.

Soon we were drinking hot sweetly spiced milky tea at a street cafe; we watched the queue for fresh lemonade at Sharah Rashid's Abu Lime kiosk. A light breeze in the air relieved the intense heat. There were shops with sweets, Turkish delight and biscuits piled into minia-ture ziggurats. Outside A.M. Soomar's Halal Printing Press we stopped to hear the sound of the old press's pistons. This Indian family had followed the British into Aden. The blue shutters and painted metal doors here were so typical of Crater, as were the wooden trestles in the street. At Bhora Bazaar we met Abdul Hussain Abdul Nabi, perfumers since 1891. The walls of his shop were an Aladdin's cave of glass-fronted cupboards holding Indian decanters, cut glass tumblers and jars, filled with amber liquids. Abdul held out his palm to us, on it sat frankincense. I took it in my hand and stared and thought; king-doms had risen and fallen because of this substance.

Back on the main street we trod a path past street traders selling dried Adeni peppers, curved like *Jambias,* and Somalis sitting in groups on tea chests weighing tobacco. Crater is still truly cosmopol-itan, a melting-pot.

We visited Obadi's bookshop and library, established in 1884. The books were heaped high, and a large encyclopaedia set sat next to the till, someone in Aden was obviously reading. Beneath whirling colo-nial fans; there was a copy of a Van Dyke painting stuck to the wall, out of place maybe, but still clinging to Western culture. The no smoking signs were unusual for Yemen, but then the shop was a potential bonfire.

After some walking, Ahmed found the old shop that his grandfather had once owned, where he grew up. It was an ample property on the corner of a dusty street. Shutters prevented strong light entering through the windows.

'I can't believe I am standing here after all this time, nothing has changed. I understand they are handing back properties to people, now that the Russians have gone, but I don't know what will happen to my family property. We will see.'

An old man tapped me on the shoulder.

'English?'

'Yes' I said.

'The English come back next year!' he said waving as he went by, with a skip in his step.

I knew that many British people had fond memories of Aden, the part of Yemen where many had lived, but it was often disliked in equal measure by those who found the climate intolerably oppressive. Aden was once considered one of the most unpleasant garrison postings in all the East India Company's possessions. The English poet and novelist, Vita Sackville-West, wrote in 1926 in *Passenger to Teheran* 'I would as soon throw myself to the sharks as live in that arid, salty hell.' But I liked Aden. I felt comfortable there.

Arthur Melville, the Scottish artist and arguably one of the greatest nineteenth-century British watercolourists arrived in Aden in 1882 and wrote

> much pleased with the place. Rugged peaked hills in the background quite like a scene on the stage. Clouds were tracking over the highest tops. The whole spectacle was more like Ben Lomond from Loch Lomond than anything tropical.

Melville, like all travellers, was making connections with his home. Yet interestingly it was not just in the mountains that he saw similarities; Scotland's largest freshwater lake, Loch Lomond was in the nineteenth century also full of piers and steamers plying the waters, just like Aden.

Many experts declare Aden to be a disaster architecturally, adding nothing to the country's vernacular tradition. But Aden was an Imperial mercantile city. It was a quiet sunny ex-colony, a place where the bees had reluctantly deserted the hive.

We moved further into Crater, to find a mosque with an attached graveyard. Ahmed's grandfather had been buried here and Ahmed had indicated to us privately that he wanted to pay his respects. Naji brought the vehicle to a halt, saying nothing. Ahmed jumped out, walked quickly across the road and disappeared through a gateway in a high wall.

'What is Ahmed doing?' asked Naji who had not been paying attention.

'He is going to the mosque,' I said.

Naji laughed.

'His grandfather is buried there.'

At last our conversation reached his ears. Naji turned his head. 'What here, in *this* place?'

'Yes.'

'Mmm,' he muttered quietly, 'This is a good thing to do.'

Yemenis are always impressed when people visit the burial place of their ancestors. For them the dead in some unexplained way can still express themselves even from their graves. Their spirits linger. We sat silently, almost painfully waiting, thinking of what was going through Ahmed's mind. The journey and arrival in Aden had already been an emotional one for him. On his return, Naji looked across at Ahmed without a word, saw him settle in his seat, turned on the engine and drove us away in silence.

We headed for the eastern end of Crater to find the ancient Tawila reservoir tanks. The Tawila tanks are the oldest construction in Aden, named after the gorge that cuts through the rocks beneath Jebel Shamsan (the mountain of two suns). This is part of a range of volcanic hills which Freya Stark wrote of in her book *The Coast of Incense* in 1953:

> There is a feeling of gigantic and naked force about it all and one thinks what it was when these hills were boiling out their steams of fire, hissing them into the sea, and wonders at anything so fragile as

man living on these ancient desolations.

The tanks, a series of eighteen cisterns carved out of solid volcanic rock, and dammed in places to take advantage of the underlying rock pattern, were originally built to give some stability in water supply to an area where several years would often pass before a heavy downpour.

We made the steep climb along the side of the tanks. They are estimated to hold 90 million litres, collecting rain from the surrounding mountains. We took some photographs of children splashing and swimming.

We drove out of the crater down into the district of Ma'alla. 1960s apartment blocks lined the main street, constrained between sea and mountain. The British had left Aden in November 1967 but the legacy of British rule was everywhere here. Passing the Rock Hotel, and the Sailors' Club, we eventually stopped at the Prince of Wales Pier in Steamer Point, almost the most western part of the peninsula. A few *dhows* and motorboats were anchored off the pier in the deep blue glistening sea and a small boat chugged by, watched by people crouching on the jetty. There was a gentle breeze. Above us on the hill behind stood the Hogg Clocktower, a miniature 'Big Ben', which is sometimes referred to as 'Little Ben.'

We walked into the Pier building. Festooned with old British signs bidding us 'Welcome to Aden,' 'Car Park', 'Exit', and 'Taxi Rank', still suspended from the roof as if nothing had changed in thirty years. This would have been the starting point for newly arrived passengers visiting Aden from ships docked in the harbour. Aden has historically been an entrepot of trade between east and west. Until the mid nineteenth century the main harbour lay on the east side of Aden at Front Bay and Holkat Bay, but with time moved to the west side into what is a truly magnificent harbour. As Captain Moti, Marketing Director of the port was to tell me later;

'There is no limit for the port of Aden. The winds and waves are all behind the Shamsan mountain range so the port is sheltered naturally. It's what we call Gods gift. We have the resources, we have the location, and we have the strategic spot that can serve both east and west. In the coming years major developments will take place as Aden becomes a free zone area. It will give the area a big push. We want to bring the good old days back to Aden.'

I tried to imagine what it must have been like to visit here even for a few hours to buy duty free goods. But the P&O ships had gone, the coal barges had disappeared, and the tens of thousands of people from all over the world, who stopped in here for a few hours while their ships refuelled to buy duty free goods had been entirely lost.

It was really rather sad. Just as Cardiff had lost its way, wondering what its function was since the demise of coal, so Aden after being in limbo for thirty years was trying to establish a new identity.

The sun blazed down as we crossed the road and wandered into an exhibition of work by local art students. For some reason it was a relief to see such contemporary creativity where young people sought and expressed influences beyond their own culture, in a place where life had stagnated under Marxist rule.

We moved on, taking photographs of the old British buildings that surrounded areas where coal would have been bunkered. Hours seemed to pass until we stopped beneath a figure of Christ, high up on a roof top, his hands raised, as if blessing the street, more reminiscent of Brazil or Argentina, than Arabia. It was the Roman Catholic Church.

'I'm sure we can go in and have a look.' said Ahmed, as we drew up outside. As we walked towards the courtyard, an Indian woman with long black plaits trailed over a starched white cotton dress came towards us. She smiled and welcomed us in as if we were members of her family.

'You want to see inside?' she said somewhat hopefully, swinging her arm towards the doorway.

'Yes Please.'

'I have a key.' she said digging deep into her pocket.

'Is the building very old?'

'It was built in 1892.'

'Do you have a priest?'

'Yes he is Indian like me.' she said smiling. 'Originally twelve sisters came here to work with refugees and lepers. Now we are here. But where are you from?'

'From Britain.'

'Oh!' Our hostess was surprised but happy.

We followed the woman into the vast interior of the church, dark and cave-like. It was a relief to get away from the strong heat of the day. After a few minutes our eyes re-adjusted to the dim light. The woman with long plaits stood in shadow as silent and still as a statue as we moved hesitantly through the aisle. At one end there was a spiral staircase, nineteenth-century ironwork, organ pipes and Victorian lamps, suspended like Christmas decorations. Our eyes wandered on to an old carved cupboard framing a Renaissance-inspired Madonna. Candles flickered in the low light, blown by the fans. The aroma of incense hung heavy in the cool space. At the east end, Jesus hung on a large cross guarded by marble angels. Muslims do not believe Jesus died on the cross, and find it difficult to understand why Christians display the instrument that killed Christ so prominently in places of worship, and even stranger that we wear the cross around our necks. Even the altar to a Muslim is a pagan symbol.

'Aden was like London before,' the Indian woman said turning up at our side. 'Many men came from India to work here. I worked in the courts before I came here. It was good then, now no good, trials used to take one month. Now they take two or three years. The new republic here took houses from the people, so all good people left Aden and we are left with the rogues. Now since unification people come back for their properties. It's getting better.' There was no self-pitying in her words, just an acceptance of history, and a wish for a better future.

'I hope you come back soon,' she said. 'The next years will be good for Aden. Our destinies are linked.'

It was time to visit the Universal Travel and Tourism offices in Aden to plan the last part of our journey. We had heard that Dhala, north of Aden was a place we could find people with British links. In the office we met Ali Dawood Ibrahim, the Aden Manager.

'So you are from Cardiff?' he said. 'I lived in Cardiff for six months in 1956, believe me I loved the discos. The atmosphere was lively.' His fit and lean physique, and rapid gestures suggested a hyperactive personality.

'I can't believe this,' said Ahmed 'everyone we meet has a relative in Cardiff...'

Naji was restless and not at all keen that we should go to Dhala which he felt might not be safe. Certainly we were adding to our original journey and we had some trouble in persuading him. In a typical Yemeni way Naji was only willing to accept the possibility of changing plans with a great deal of debate. As with many Arabs, there was a passionate conflict between his sense of individual freedom and loyalty to his travelling companions. We discussed the positive and the negative sides of the argument for travelling to Dhala, but the possibility of finding people there with British links was compelling. Accepting the opinion of the three of us, Naji made a few phone calls back to the head office in Sana'a, and anyhow his curiosity was finally getting the better of him. Over a drink of coffee a big grin spread across his face;

'No problem... we go to Dhala.' The matter was settled and there was no ill-will.

Meanwhile a man in his early thirties entered the office and listened to our conversation before speaking in Arabic to Ahmed.

'This man says we ought to meet a member of the Al-Hakimi family who lives in Sheikh Othman. He is the brother of the man Taha Muhammed told you about in the British Embassy in Sana'a. His father had important connections with Cardiff. He is getting his telephone number for us, we will phone him and see if we can visit him,' said Ahmed.

The man, like a message-carrying angel disappeared as quickly as he had arrived.

Hamoud al-Hakimi, Sheikh Othman

Echoes from the Past

'A man who does not leave home will learn nothing.'
(Welsh proverb)

Ahmed made a call and we headed for Sheikh Othman, a satellite town to the west of Aden, congested with people. We stopped by an area of pottery workshops where the wares spilled out on to the road, and asked directions to Hakimi's house.

'Number 76... here it is,' said Ahmed as we drove up outside.

We stood with Ahmed as he pushed open a pale green courtyard door, and knocked confidently on another. After a few minutes a small, gracefully-robed women appeared. We exchanged courtesies and stumbled up some very steep stairs.

At the top we entered into a bright green room. A set of fan shaped coloured glass windows, of burgundy red, royal blue and emerald green, let in a rainbow light. There was an air of decaying gentility. As our eyes adjusted to the light we saw the short figure of Hamoud al-Hakimi rising from a set of cushions.

'Welcome to my house,' he said. 'Please sit.'

Hakimi's wife brought us tea on a tray, and we sat and supped while Ahmed explained our undertaking. Soon we realised our host was becoming excited. He was delighted that we had come to Aden, all the way from Cardiff. He pointed to a framed picture hanging on the wall. I stood up and went closer to it. It was the cover of a magazine, with a portrait painting of an Arab. Written in large letters the title *Today* was spread across the top and underneath the words 'Imam of the Cardiff Mosque.' It looked early 1950s.

'That is my father,' said Hakimi.

'You two don't just have connections with Yemen, part of your history is here.' said Ahmed to us staring at the image and shaking his head in disbelief. It was a statement of shared identity so loved by Yemenis. Somehow our 'ancestry' had a common history. We had been travelling to new places but all we were finding was confirmation of connections with home.

It reminded me of an incident described by Harold Ingrams in his 1942 book *Arabia and the Isles*. He was asked by one eighty-one year old man from Hajjarain whether he came from London. Ingrams explained that he came from another town. The old man asked 'Cardiff?'

'No not Cardiff' replied Ingrams.

Persisting the old man said 'If it wasn't London it must be Cardiff.'

'Why?' asked Ingrams 'there are more towns in England' (Ingrams writes that Wales was too difficult to explain).

'No,' replied the old man. 'There are only two towns in England, London and Cardiff. My son lives in Cardiff but has been to London and he has never mentioned any other place. You must be wrong. My son says England is an island and London and Cardiff are its towns.'

Given that this was written so long ago and that Ingrams' interlocutor was in his eighties it must be a fair description of how many Yemenis viewed Britain.

I handed Hamoud the cutting from the newspaper Taha Muhammed had given me in Sana'a. Hamoud read it slowly.

'Ah yes this was my brother, he died recently.'

'It mentions Cardiff in the article?'

'My father was a great man, he was a great man you know,' said Hamoud with emphasis, 'for his sons, for his country and his people.'

'What was his name?' I asked.

'Sheikh Abdullah Ali al-Hakimi. He was against our past government, Imam Ahmed and his father Yahya, because he thought they were tyrants. My father wanted to change everything. For things to become like Britain, for Yemen to become a democracy. He once worked as a sailor, like so many men in those days. Working on ships as stokers, sailing around the world. But he was different, he didn't just stay a sailor. He had religious leanings, and wanted to pursue them.'

'How did he do that?'

'After he finished as a sailor he joined a Sufi sect, a form of mystical Islam known as the Allawi Shadhlili sect. In 1926 he left Aden, and went to Algeria. There he stayed for a while and studied. He took up learning, literature, the language, Islamic studies and developed so much that he was nominated to go to France to be an instructor in the ways of the faith. Many Yemenis in those days went to France, they travelled to Djibouti and on to ships that sailed for Marseilles. But he didn't stay there long, only about six months. He found it hard amongst the French people. So he travelled on to Holland and stayed there for two years. Some of the Yemeni sailors he met told him it was better for him to go to Britain, the British people were more understanding and free, more democratic he was told.'

'Did he travel to Cardiff or London?'

'Neither, he first travelled to South Shields in 1936 where there was a large Yemeni community.'

He founded the Zawiya Islamia Allawia Religious Society of the United Kingdom, a religious brotherhood, and secured funds for small mosques (zawiyas) in the UK. In South Shields he concentrated on religious issues, creating a religious revival, and also promoted Islamic education for women and children, including the British wives of the many Yemenis.

'He then was invited down to Tiger Bay in Cardiff in 1938. He worked there in the mosque and established a society for Yemenis in Cardiff and looked after their problems. He was paid from the wages of the sailors. One of his achievements, with the help of other Yemenis, was to build the first purpose-built mosque in Wales,' said Hamoud.

I found out on my return to Wales that, in an interview in the *Western Mail* in 1938, Sheikh Abdullah al-Hakimi revealed his intention to settle in the city.

> It is my ambition to found a mosque in Cardiff. In this city alone there are some 5,000 members of our faith, and the only place in which they can worship at present is a room at the premises occupied by the Zawiya Allawia Friendship Society in Bute Street. Of course, the Arab population in Cardiff is a shifting one, for many of the Arabs spend the greater part of their time at sea. Those residing in Cardiff, however, meet for prayers five times a day.'

The lodging house and shop in Bute Street, in which this first place of worship was located was owned by Sayyid Hashim. Then the community bought some dilapidated houses in nearby Peel Street which were converted into a temporary mosque, but this was bombed by the Germans during the war. The Cardiff Yemeni Community raised funds for a mosque by writing letters to people, including Sir Bernard Reilly, the Governor of Aden. The Colonial Office in Aden also supported the building of the mosque.

The Nur-al-Islam Mosque in Peel Street was eventually completed in 1944 at a cost of £7,000. The community, including Sheikh Said's adoptive father Sheikh Hassan Ismail, was responsible for much of the work. They then followed this with one of the first Muslim cemeteries in Britain (previously Muslims were buried beside Christians), and facilities for Arabic language teaching. The daily religious life of these Muslims and other duties such as the giving of alms and fasting, were now focused around the mosque. The establishment of a place to worship meant that Islamic festivals like 'Id al-Fitr' (The Feast of Breaking the Fast) at the end of Ramadan, and 'Id al-Adha' (The Feast of Sacrifice) which signalled the end of the pilgrimage to Mecca, could also be celebrated.

Hamood continued to tell us that his father Abdullah became increasingly political and campaigned for democracy in Yemen from his base in Cardiff. This was at a time when the whole Arab World was increasingly focusing on politics, and a new class of intellectuals was emerging in Aden and Yemen. Sheikh Abdullah hated what he saw as the harshness of the Imam's rule, although he was not against the rule of constitutional monarchs on the British model in 1939. But he abhorred the British presence in Aden. In fact he returned to Aden, which was frowned upon by many in the Cardiff Yemeni community who had volunteered for the war effort. Leaving Britain during its hour of need made it look as if he had fled, some said.

I thought of Sheikh Hassan Ismail, Sheikh Said's adoptive father, who had been Sheikh Abdullah's deputy in Cardiff for some time. They disagreed in their attitudes towards Imam Ahmed, of North Yemen and went their separate ways. Sheikh Hassan did not leave Britain during the Second World War, but rallied the Yemenis to fight in the war effort and support Britain against fascism.

Taha at the British Embassy had told us that Hakimi was one of the leading figures in the nationalist opposition movement of Free Yemenis along with Sheikh Muhammad Zubairi and Sheikh Ahmed No'man. They had been living in Egypt and returned to North Yemen with new progressive ideas, but were imprisoned. They were eventually released and fled to Aden. Sheikh Abdullah Al-Hakimi was expelled from Taiz in 1943 by the Crown Prince Ahmed for being a member of the Free Yemenis who since the late 1930s had been organising opposition to Imam Yahya. Their manifesto was circulating in the UK by 1941. Yemenis who had found employment on ships in the port of Aden or in Europe and America could not fail to criticise the poor and backward conditions of Yemen which had resulted from the policy of isolationism pursued by Imam Yahya to keep the colonial powers in the region at bay. There were no decent roads, hospitals, schools. Foreign newspapers and radios were banned. The taxation burden imposed by the Imam, his governors and soldiers, on the Shafi'is in the southern highlands was a great incentive to emigrate. Old Yemenis in Cardiff had told me that the Imam's soldiers came into the villages and stole their livestock.

After the Second World War, Sheikh Abdullah returned to Britain and began publishing one of the first Arabic newspapers in the country, the *Al-Salam* (peace) newspaper (a fortnightly in Arabic) from the Nur-al-Islam Mosque, Peel Street, in Butetown Cardiff. It was funded by his supporters in Aden, and the paper was distributed in Britain, North Africa and the Middle East. It was a main voice of dissent against the ruling Imam between 1948 and the mid 1950s as opposition and dissatisfaction in the Yemen grew.

'My father could not have spoken out like this in the colony of Aden, they would not have allowed it, but in Cardiff he was free to do what ever he wanted.' said Hamoud.

The Free Yemenis formed the Grand Yemeni Association in Aden in January 1946, and the Yemeni community in Cardiff were the first to support it. Sheikh Abdullah also called on the British Government to support it. When Imam Ahmed succeeded Yahya, after his father's assassination in 1948, he did what he could to destroy Sheikh

Abdullah, whom he believed was being supported by the British financially, although there is no evidence for this.

Feuding began between various groups in Cardiff, supporters of the Free Yemenis led by Sheikh Abdullah and supporters of the Imam, led by Sheikh Hassan Ismail. It is possible that the support for various groups was along tribal lines as much as anything else. The Shamiris supported Sheikh Hassan Ismail and were the largest tribal group among the seamen in Britain.

Hamoud explained how, at the age of fourteen, he had worked in Cardiff on the press of *Al-Salam*.

'Cardiff was where we could breath. We were treated like sons of Wales, not like foreigners. My father wanted freedom, education and development of the economy. In the newspaper published in Cardiff, he could criticise both the Imam and the British. But he basically appreciated the British democratic system...in Britain itself, but not the system in the colonies.'

This interest in democracy, even in Aden and the Protectorates, was addressed by Sir Tom Hickinbotham, who became governor of Aden in 1951, and who personally knew Sheikh Abdullah. In his book *Aden*, he says;

> In Aden Colony there are 38,000 Arabs from the Protectorate in close contact with a democratic form of government, many of whom exercise their voting right when elections to the Legislative and Municipal Councils take place. These people have become accustomed to a democratic system of government, not only in Aden, but also in countries in the West to which many of them travel. When they return to their Protectorate homes, which many of them do at frequent intervals, they find the old-fashioned autocratic rule of their Sheikh or Sultan irksome. They would like at home what they have become used to abroad, an ever-increasing say in the government of the country. At present these people are in the minority, but it will not be long before the wish of the few becomes the demand of the majority, and the wisest of the Protectorate Rulers are ready and willing to accept change and bow before the inevitable.

In the *Al-Salam* newspaper, which was smuggled into what was then North Yemen, Hakimi wrote that Yemenis should be able to build an economy with such fertile land and a large population, and did not need to send their people all over the world to make money. He had a vision of a stable and wealthy Yemen.

Al-Salam kept Yemenis aware of the outside world and expatriate Yemenis aware of what was happening inside the country. This was all taking place in the context of the rise of republicanism in the Arab world encouraged by Nasser's Egypt.

'My father left Cardiff to travel to Aden in 1952; two of his friends were in prison in Yemen at that time' said Hamoud reflecting, and lowering the tone of his voice. 'He returned to Aden to support the people there and set up a newspaper, but I believe it proved difficult as it affected British relations with the Yemeni government in the North. On his arrival in Aden, Sheikh Abdullah spoke at a huge rally, saying there was no justice in Yemen. Because of this, he said, Yemenis were scattered across the world and were losing their culture and identity.'

A few days later he was charged with being in possession of a revolver when entering the colony. He was arrested and imprisoned for a year. He was released in the following July declaring his innocence and his support for British democratic traditions. The blame for the gun has been been laid at the door of everyone imaginable, as has his death. He died in 1954 of suspected poisoning, at the age of 63.

Woman by a doorway

Crossing The Divide

'When you travel you find out who your friends are.'
(Arab proverb)

We headed north out of Aden and passed over the old but still manned border between the North and South. It was Yemen's Checkpoint Charlie. The police stopped us and Naji was asked to show his licence. A little further on they tried to stop us again, but Naji decided to ignore them and drive on. As far as he was concerned we had already dealt with the formalities but the police took another view altogether and started waving their guns in the air and shouting.

'Stop, Naji, stop!' shouted Charles, looking back, worried at what might happen next. Naji stopped. The police came up to the vehicle, yelling and wanted to book Naji. But when they saw us in the back, and read the letter from the Ministry of Culture and Tourism which Ahmed brought out of his bag, they waved us on.

We were heading for Dhala, a small town just inside the old north-south border, where we were told we could find some British Yemenis. The town is not a very interesting place, lying on the side of a hill, covered by groups of small terraced farms, the centre itself somewhat worn and weary, but the most interesting people often live in the most difficult regions.

On arriving we booked into the only hotel in town. Like the Crescent in Aden, no one seemed to be staying there. The man behind reception, learning about our research, stared at us as if we were mad, coming to Dhala, but said 'I know Cardiff. I lived there for four years between 1983 and 1986, I have visited Cardiff many times.' Ahmed's mouth dropped, as a group of men gathered around us. One sporting a Birmingham accent another a Liverpudlian, with quite a respectable Beatles haircut.

'If I went to the embassy do you think they would give me a passport? I lived in Britain for 25 years,' said one.

They spent time asking us about home. What was the news over the past few years? It felt rather strange being surrounded by the regional accents of Britain in such a remote place rarely visited by outsiders. It was another moment when we realised how much Yemenis knew about Britain, but how little we knew about them.

We were all tired. It had been a long and winding road, and Naji was not happy about being in territory he did not know well or understand. We all went to our rooms. It was very hot, and at first we kept the window open. But realising that there were kamikaze mosquitoes everywhere, we closed the window. It made no difference. We spent half the night awake. Some were hiding behind the headboard of the bed and others snuggled into the curtain folds. Every time we relaxed they took their chance and bombarded us. We did catch a few, and when we did we cheered as if we had conquered some great adversary.

When we met Ahmed and Naji the next morning we realised we had been lucky. They looked as white as ghosts.

'I only slept one hour,' said Naji. 'Mosquitoes!' He said waving his arms in the air.

'It's the opposite,' said Ahmed. 'He slept and I didn't.' And so they argued.

We drove into the dirty, uninteresting market place in Dhala. The only mesmerising sight was a woman covered in turmeric – as if covered in war paint – to protect her skin from the sun. War was more visible on a nearby wall. Here, like the insignia in Aden, was a mural dating from the 1960s. It was faded but just visible enough to make out the subject matter. Unlike the tribute to the South Wales Borderers it showed the capture of a British soldier by nationalists. It was a sad reminder of more difficult days. But most young Yemenis that we were now meeting regarded those days as part of a shared history, a history consigned to the past. New relationships were being forged. One Yemeni journalist told me a joke:

There was a qat chewing session. A group of Yemeni men were sitting in a mafraj, as they chewed they discussed their problems. 'What are we going to do with the country now it is unified and we need money to organise it?' said one throwing the idea across the room. Everyone was silent. A man from the back of the room spoke up 'We could declare war on the British... then they could come back for fifteen years, and sort everything out.' Everyone around the room nodded in agreement until a small voice piped up from the back of the room and said; 'But what if we won?

As we drove out of Dhala on to some remote roads we saw a boy on the back of a vehicle, who was fair-skinned with light-brown curly hair.

'He looks half and half,' I said.

'What?' said Ahmed.

'You know half and half – half Arab, half European, perhaps British, perhaps even Russian.'

Ahmed looked inquisitively and agreed he certainly didn't look local. He hailed the vehicle to stop and called to the boy. Soon we discovered that his mother was English and living nearby.

'I can't believe that an English woman is living here,' said Ahmed 'He is inviting us to his house, do you want to go?'

'Of course,' I said knowing that we could not miss meeting any English woman living in such a remote part of Yemen.

Margaret came to the front door of her modest two-storey stone house. She gasped and gave us a lingering look. Dressed in a bright red chiffon headscarf and red and grey floral dress, a bunch of keys hung around her neck like an amulet. She spoke softly and invited us up her narrow staircase, into the family room. We reclined against the wall on cushions. Some of her children gathered around us.

'How did you find me?' she asked earnestly.

'We were just driving along the road and spotted your son.'

'I haven't seen anyone from Britain for twenty years,' she said.

Margaret explained to us that she had come from West Bromwich in the early 70s with her three children and Yemeni husband, and never left.

'My husband is a magistrate. So we have lived in this place for what seems forever.' Her eyes looked across at Ahmed; she swallowed and continued. 'When I first arrived, I couldn't understand anyone and found the food terrible. Everything seemed strange. I wanted to go home, but I couldn't leave my children.' It didn't take much imagination, to understand Margaret's situation.

'Yes, it was difficult at first. I was an outsider and the local people didn't accept me. Pulling water from a well, cooking over a wood-fired oven, speaking the language, it was all so difficult.'

'Do you have family in England?' I asked.

'Yes, I missed my mother the most, but when she died, I thought what was the point of going home. By then I had been here so long I began to accept this place as home – there was no reason to return.'

'So you have many friends here now.'

'I have made friends now, especially with an older woman here, Naema, who has replaced my mother. She is a great comfort to me, and understands me. Her husband worked on the British ships as a seaman and we really understand each other.'

'You have more than three children now,' I said smiling and looking around us.

Without constraint she said, 'Yes, I've given birth to thirteen children here... on this floor... only with hot water' she said lifting her eyes, 'although only ten survived. I had to read up about medicine, there was no doctor here. Those whom I did meet did not even look at my children; they said 'go to the chemist and buy what you like.' The first doctor I saw after arriving in Yemen couldn't even help with my children's diarrhoea.'

After this experience Margaret became a local nurse in the community she lived in, dispensing simple medicines and dressing wounds and injuries that occurred in the village. She gained respect.

'Don't you want to go back to England to visit?' I said.

'My husband visits the UK every few years, but I have not been there. What is it like now?'

I stared at her, not knowing how to reply. I tried to visualise what changes must have taken place over the past twenty years. I could have said we were getting more affluent but more miserable, but then that might have upset her. We spoke about Shakespeare and inner-city development. She was spontaneous and free in her spirit despite her situation. We discussed home as best we could for someone who had been out of touch with everything save her local Yemeni community.

'There was no piped water here until four years ago.' she said. 'Can you believe that?... and no electricity until ten years ago.'

There was a sound of people chattering, children shouting. Suddenly through the door came a man carrying a bag and papers. It was Margaret's husband. In the short time we had been sitting in the house, he had been contacted by some locals who had seen us. He apparently thought we might have been relatives. Other men arrived. They had lived in Sheffield, and they all filed into the room filling it with laughter and warm conversation.

We left Margaret and her friends and were heading for Haifan, Ahmed's ancestral village, just over the old border. Ahmed seemed nervous but happy. We wound through rugged mountain passes and along rough donkey tracks. Single storey buildings were scattered along the valley sides in the distance, so small they resembled piles of bricks left out to dry. Ahmed's home appeared, hugging the edge of a hill, and we wound our way up to the entrance. It was a stone house set neatly in the village. His mother came out to greet us, as Naji parked the Toyota in a safe place. She gave Ahmed a huge hug and they exchanged an elaborate series of courtesies, made by Yemenis when they meet, especially when they have not seen each other for some time. Then we shook hands with her and were led inside to the *mafraj*. After waiting for a few minutes we were led into a side room, where Ahmed's father sat in a wheelchair. We greeted him and he smiled gently at us, and then turned his head towards the window. Tea was brought on a tray with cups as neatly laid out as a Chardin still life. Ahmed's mother sat down with us. She was excited to see her son and obviously proud of him. Few people held a responsible position in a Ministry as he did. He had left this house as a child to live in Aden with his grandfather, who traded there. Our visit to Aden had been emotional for him. Few people re-visited their old homes and haunts at this time. The newly-united government later began handing back properties that had been seized and nationalised by the Marxist regime. After unification in May 1990 many people working in the public sector were given jobs in different parts of the country in an attempt to unite the two parts psychologically and socially as well as on paper. With different political, economic and cultural backgrounds this was an enormous challenge. Aden was now free to trade with the world again, but it had been forgotten as other ports in the Gulf region had expanded. Iraq had recently invaded Kuwait and around one million Yemenis working in the Gulf had returned home.

Ahmed's mother must have had this on her mind as she turned towards Naji and asked 'Are you Kuwaiti?'

'No, *mumkin* (maybe) he's Saudi,' said Charles, teasing.

'No! Saudi me?' said Naji merrily. 'Me Yemeni, *min Yarim*, Yemeni!' Identity was crucial to Naji particularly having lived abroad. He understood his home, Yemen, better because of his travels.

Ahmed's mother turned to Charles and myself.

'Are you brother and sister?'

'No,' said Naji laughing back at us. ' They are husband and wife.'

'Everyone says this on the road' said Ahmed.

There was a rapid exchange in Arabic. Ahmed looked across at us laughing.

'What is happening?' I asked.

'Naji has just said to my mother, that we started out on this journey as strangers, but now we are brothers. He said we have travelled together, eaten together, laughed together and most importantly we have argued and shouted at each other – so now we must be friends.'

It reminded me of the old Yemeni proverb 'When you travel you find out who your friends are.' Certainly we had argued and debated all-day long for nearly five weeks. It was a healthy sign. We all develop in communication with other human beings. In Yemen people express their views on all different kinds of subjects much more freely than in many Arab countries, and as in Wales, particularly the Welsh Valleys, there is a tendency for friends to speak with unusual candour.

Old stoker, Naje Ali Abdullah – Shamir

Do You Know Anyone From Cardiff?

> 'We could talk about shipping in Liverpool and
> Cardiff and many Asiatic harbours, for strangely
> enough many of these inland Arabs are sailors.
> Five hundred men were at sea from one valley
> alone, solitary and sunburned and surrounded by
> the desert. They are mostly stokers; the engine
> rooms of ships are probably not unpleasant to
> anyone born to the climate of South Arabia.'
>
> (Freya Stark: *East is West*)

'**D**o you know anyone from Cardiff?' shouted Naji as he paced
up and down in the street. The sooner we managed to find
some people to talk to the quicker Naji could get back in the Toyota
and drive us on to our next destination during daylight. It was true
that driving at night in Yemen was hazardous.

We knew that some men from south of the provincial capital Taiz,
had emigrated to Aden but most of those with connections with
Wales come from west of Taiz. We were still diligently seeking out
British Yemenis, who had retired home.

They generally came from the same families and tribes. The most
prominent tribe who came for employment in Cardiff and other
south Wales ports were the Shamiris. What tribe you are from, was
and usually still is, more important than the fact that you are a
Yemeni. We drove for some hours, negotiating routes driving north.
Two storey buildings now turned to fortified three or four storey
buildings as we headed inland.

We were directed towards Hagdah, a small hamlet known for
producing one of the best cheeses in Yemen. We stopped for tea at a

small cafe. Naji's determination to get back into the driving seat meant that he rushed through the market trying to find some people for us to speak too. Mr M.K. Mokbil had coincidentally been walking down the street, and responded to Naji's call. Within minutes he was sitting next to Charles in the cafe where we had already caused something of a stir. There was a twinkle in his eye.

'Hello, welcome to Yemen,' he said in a broad Welsh accent. 'I am from Swansea.'

'Yes he is a Swansea man, a Swansea man,' shouted one of the others, following him in.

Mr Mokbil sat down and explained he had travelled to Swansea and spent forty years, on and off, sailing the open seas on ships to places as far away as Australia. He had even been to Japan and America and had spent many weekends in Cardiff with his cousin who lived in Bute Street.

'What did you do?' I asked.

'I was a stoker like so many men from here. Whole villages left this area to work on coal ships.'

'Was it hard work?' I asked knowing it was at least dirty and hot.

'Oh hard work is not the name for it – it brought sweat and tears. There would be six of us in the engine room. Two at a time, one English, one Yemeni – four hour shifts. We would throw coal into the fire and then after it burned we would have to clean out. This was difficult. We had to take ash, and then run up on to the top of the ship and throw it overboard. We worked hard, we were exhausted. But I saw the world. If I was young I would go back and live in Cardiff or Swansea,' he said with a cheeky smile.

The work of these men was intensive. Like miners in a pit, working in the darkness of a stoke-hole could be suffocating. The stoke-hole was hot and lacked any ventilation. A ship may need to carry three thousand tons of coal for a single voyage. As much as twenty or thirty tons an hour needed to be shovelled into the fire. The furnace doors may at times be only a little wider than the shovel, and the coal had to be spread around the fire and thrown to the back. The fitness of these men became legendary. The coal was stored in waterproof bunkers near the stoke-hole and brought to the stoker by a trimmer, who would have to work in darkness with only the light of a safety-lamp amidst piles of coal which at any moment could be displaced by the motion of the ship. The conditions were dirty and hot. Wet coal was a disaster, as steam-smoke often covered the men, when they tried to clean out the furnace slag on to the stoke-hole floor. Working four hour shifts as Mr Mokbil did meant that often you only slept for a few hours in between, and a twelve hour day was not unusual. It was possible to work 84-hour weeks for weeks or months. Over the boiler was a steam pressure gauge which could be read at all times. It was an art to keep the pressure of steam up – by knowing when to shovel in the coal. To much or too little steam was a problem.

We were joined by more men, accidentally passing, or some collected by enthusiastic locals, who had never seen westerners in their village before. All of them generous and welcoming. A few of them frail. There was a lot of to-ing and fro-ing. The people running the cafe moved chairs and tables, brought juice, and soon stories were coming thick and fast. Conversation revolved around the engine rooms of coal ships. It was pure nostalgia.

Abdul Galil Abdo Hassan worked out of Cardiff for over ten years and then London for twenty. He started as a stoker on the coal ships in 1950. Next to him sat Faid Kahtan who lived in the Cardiff docklands and knew Sheikh Said.

'The City of Cardiff, like London or Liverpool is well known to many Yemenis. As someone said to me in Aden 'we all know somebody who was a stoker or seaman who went to Britain'.'

The lodging house was the centre of all the activities in the Arab communities in South Wales and other ports in Britain. Since the nineteenth century a seaman was required to stay in a licensed lodging house, rather than a private house. These houses had to be inspected and approved, and follow certain hygiene and other regulations. It provided food cooked by Islamic law, and offered rooms for the five daily prayers, until the small mosque or zawiya was established. The lodging house owner would also help in finding work with their links with seamen's agents in Aden and would even lend money or extend credit to sailors waiting to find work. Some lodging houses even sent money back to Yemen on behalf of seamen.

Everything in the lodging houses was taken on trust. The Yemeni sailors would often hang around for a few months, making friends, playing dominoes, reciting stories and competing with each other with jokes, poems and proverbs while trying to find work on a ship. Armed with their dispatch books they would go out looking for a ship to employ them. During the wars there was plenty of work. It was a close-knit community where you might not see a merchant seaman for some time; he maybe owed you quite a bit of money. Hinda Awad, a Welsh Yemeni, said her father wielded considerable influence with the seamen, but he also expected loyalty in return. He would often wait maybe months, even years, to be re-paid for lodging bills or loans. During the economic depression of the inter-war period, however, some problems did arise as Arab seamen were laid off work, and although Yemen has traditionally had a support system within its tribal groups, some bitter rivalries did develop between the various lodging houses and families within the Yemeni communities in Britain. Some of these rivalries continue to this day. At the same time white British sailors in post-war Britain were competing with Arabs for jobs. Many had been paid less for fighting in the war than Arabs had been paid for working on the ships, and felt that the Arabs should go home with their earnings. Also Arab firemen on ships were paid a comparable wage to a British fireman. Most Arabs knew that they had been loyal to Britain in time of war. All this caused racial tensions, as did Arab seamen dating local women. There were serious disturbances in a number of ports including Cardiff which left three people dead. In those days 'Tiger Bay' was often seen by many Cardiff residents as a dockland ghetto, and not a very safe one at that, but to locals like Sheikh Said it was a friendly place where different nationalities mostly mixed in relative harmony.

Olive Salaman, who ran the 'Cairo Cafe,' a lodging house in Cardiff, with her husband Ali became known locally as the 'mother of the Yemenis' and remembers much kindness during the war. British women who had married Yemeni men often became key intermediary figures between the sailors and the local community. Although at first there was no way Arabs living in Britain could marry according to Muslim law, this soon changed and we know that Sheikh Hassan Ismail and Sheikh

Abdullah Ali al-Hakimi (who married Olive and Ali) possessed licences to conduct marriages conforming to Islamic law.

Olive, like many British women who married Yemenis, became a Muslim. With Ali she had ten children and later nursed many old sailors, who were dying in her care. One old Yemeni's last request was for an apple to eat, but there was not an apple in the shop, it was wartime, and rationing was on. An American ship had just docked that day and men were coming in for meals. Olive asked them if they could help with apples for the old dying Yemeni. The next day a complete box was dropped off by the American sailors at the lodging house.

Wadi Said a seaman, poet and cultural officer for the Yemeni Community Association in Cardiff, who served in both the Falklands War and Bosnia, is the third generation of his family to have travelled the world by ship. 'You have to learn how to save the ship and people,' he said to me. His grandfather died on a torpedoed ship and his father Abdul Said almost died the same way in the Second World War when his ship was hit in the Mediterranean. With his friend Abdul Gabber he survived on a wooden raft for eight hours in the sea before being picked up by another British ship. Five Yemeni friends died that day on the ship. Writing poems about his experience he described how coming back to Wales was like coming to a place with 'good weather.'

Naji Ali Abdullah claimed to be over 100 years of age. He told me he remembered the riots over work and race relations that erupted in South Shields during 1919, in which he temporarily was caught up as the ship he was working on was docked there. He was wiry in stature, blind in one eye, wore a scarf over his shoulder, and held a plastic bag in his hands. Like many stokers his hands had been burnt. He looked like an aged athlete. To be a stoker you had to be very fit. He told me that he was docked in Marseilles when the First World War broke out, which was not unusual for a Yemeni as the Messageries Maritimes Steam Navigation Company of France, was the largest shipping company in the world and had its headquarters there. It used Aden as a re-fuelling station on its way to Shanghai, and often recruited staff there. Other Yemenis had travelled to nearby Djibouti which was occupied by France in 1884 and along with their Somali neighbours (who unlike mountain Yemenis often had seafaring experience on *dhows*) travelled to Europe via Suez and Port Said from where they obtained jobs on British ships. In fact this route was so well known that numerous cultures interwove with each other. Dr David Jenkins, curator of the Maritime Collection at the National Museums and Galleries of Wales told me one such story. The captain of a ship from Holyhead in North Wales was sailing through the Suez Canal to Port Said. In those days bum-boatsmen would energetically sell produce from small rowing boats beneath the gigantic hulls of the ships. On this particular day the bum-boats were getting in the way and being a nuisance. The Welsh-speaking captain starting yelling derogatory names at the Arabs below. In a flash one of the bum-boatmen shouted back in Welsh. Shocked, the captain started a conversation, only to find out that the Arab had worked with many Welsh speakers on board ships out of North Wales.

'Our ship left Marseilles and we went to Cardiff to get coal,' Naji Ali continued 'I worked in the engine room, stoking. I can remember queuing for days in the Bristol Channel waiting to dock. We needed the fine quality steam coal. Bad coal is like flour, when you throw it on the fire. It won't burn.'

He went on to explain... 'When we docked we looked out and all we could see were mountains of coal. I left the ship then, which was rare, we usually stayed on board. I can see the Glamorgan Canal and Queen Street even now.'

I was amazed to be sitting in a remote village in Yemen with an old sailor telling me things about Cardiff that even I didn't know. He visited around my great grandfather's time as a coal leveller and I thought for a moment that they could have walked within a few metres of each other as they waited for a ship to be loaded. Sometimes coal was on board ship being handled by Yemeni seamen within 48 hours of being dug out of the ground by miners up the valleys.

'How long did you work like this?' I continued.

'I worked on ships for over fifty years, often I did not go ashore in years, believe me that was the way life was. Once I stayed on the ship for five years, honest. Never touching dry ground. But in Cardiff I went ashore.'

Ships' crews had an agreement to behave properly, on board and ashore. On a ship's document I later saw it stated 'the crew agree to conduct themselves in an orderly, faithful honest and sober manner, and to be at all times diligent in their respective duties and to be obedient to the lawful commands of the said Master...'

Naji Ali continued, 'I travelled everywhere – Japan, Europe, Australia, and in 1917 I went to New York. The weather was terrible, the sea was churning, so bad we thought the ship was going to break up. But good coal can get you quickly out of bad weather. The storm got worse and waves were lashing high. I went to my room to pray to Allah. The captain came to find me, he was very upset and asked me what I thought I was doing and why I was not in the engine room maintaining a good head of steam. I went back to the engine room and we worked hard to save the ship. You know it's not true what they say about the captain being the last off the ship. It was always the stokers – they had to keep the ship running.'

Crossing the Atlantic with its rough seas and long distances was a great challenge for steamships. Churchill said that one of his greatest worries in the Second World War was the defeat of the Atlantic convoys by the U-boats. Many Yemenis were responsible alongside British, Commonwealth and Empire men for sustaining the effort to defeat Hitler and win the war.

Captain Jac Alun, a seaman from a family of Welsh-speaking poets from Y Cilie farm near Llangranog in West Wales, spent over thirty-nine years travelling the world and wrote that on one Cardiff ship he worked for there were forty-eight crew and sixteen were Arabs. They were given a special place for prayer on ship but it always amazed the British how the Arabs could find the direction of Mecca. No doubt even the British sailors at times had difficulty knowing what direction the ship was going in, but many Arabs even as late as the beginning of this century had a detailed knowledge of the stars. Of course this was only useful if there was a cloudless sky. Jac Alun remembers telling one Arab sailor that when he was a child in Sunday School in Wales they used to pray 'Oh God remember the Arabs who sleep under the stars' but unfortunately this Arab was not happy that Christians were praying for him. Jac Alun wrote of one Ali Mohammad, an Arab working on ship who went to help the captain after the ship was hit by a mine and in trouble. He swore he would not leave him saying 'I'll stay by you Sir.' He eventually carried him to safety and was given a BEM – a British Empire Medal for his courage.

Yemenis have always been used to sailing in difficult weather conditions. Winds and currents meant that there were particular sailing seasons between the main ports in the early days of sailing. The medieval Arab traveller Ibn Battuta wrote that at night ships did not travel because of the many sandbars, reefs and strong currents. Numerous shipwrecks are found along the Arabian coast, even the explorer Richard Burton was nearly lost at sea here.

'I worked between Cardiff and Aden originally.' said Naji Ali 'Before this I fought against the British with the Turks.' Naji Ali Abdullah claimed with a smile to have a pension. I continued listening intently, aware that we were bystanders, visitors just passing through, but an important link to something in their past.

'Bad coal gives you trouble.' murmured Omar Hassan who maintained he was in his mid-eighties. 'Can't sleep, can't eat, hard work – everything too hard. Some coal good, some coal bad. Different coals – south Welsh, good coal on the fire. Another coal very bad, gives you trouble – damp and makes smoke and does not give steam.'

Yemenis claim good coal never gave them ash. 'China, India, South Africa coal no good. Welsh coal the best. You could use it and rest, even relax, it burned slowly and the steam was good.' He said he hated the waters around the British coastline; it was rough, and made him sick and crossing the Atlantic was no mean feat. At least with a sailing ship the sails would balance and hold the ship steady on the water. The steamship did not have this advantage and could even run straight into a wind which a sailing ship did not do.

It was in these difficult waters and on these long journeys that masters of steamers apparently favoured Yemeni firemen, as they are correctly known. It was usual at the time to call a man a stoker in the Royal Navy where it was a rank and a fireman in the Merchant Navy, but later both terms were used. They were hard working, full of stamina, rarely drunk in port, and were willing to do overtime without extra pay.

Abdul Mohammed Abdullah said he was seventy-four years old

and was involved in the war. He left Aden in 1941 – as a stoker.

'I worked with the convoys in the Second World War. Those jobs were important to us, we had money, we could travel the world. But we had to do our jobs well.'

Many British tramp steamers were forced under the control of the Ministry of Shipping to abandon their normal routes and form convoys led by naval ships.

Abdul Nasser Abdul grinned. He was a stoker during the Second World War.

'I went to Liverpool and started work on a ship. I worked as a stoker, a donkey man and a fireman. On the way to Gibraltar there were eight ships in our convoy but a torpedo hit us. I survived but lost two men from my ship. Fishing boats rescued us. Eight ships were sunk. I survived, many didn't.'

I realised that leaving Yemen had been a great sacrifice for many of these men, especially during the First and Second World Wars. In the Book of Remembrance at the Maritime Museum in Halifax, Nova Scotia an Ahmed Said, a fireman, age 26 from Aden is recorded as having died on a Cardiff-registered ship the SS *Picton* (named after Sir Thomas Picton, Wellington's Welsh General). Five other Muslims also died on the ship – Ahmed Ali, Caleb Ghanin, Mohammed Birit, Mohammed Bashir, and A. Saleh. The Halifax explosion was caused by the SS *Mont Blanc*, a munitions ship that had arrived from New York to join a convoy. It was the greatest explosion of the First World War and the largest man-made explosion until the dropping of the bomb at Hiroshima in 1945.

Working in these tough conditions, when they could have been back home farming, involved a degree of risk and loneliness. But Yemen was, and still is, a poor country in economic terms, and its economy was failing. Before the revolution started in the north, in 1962, there were few jobs in Yemen outside the village except to become a soldier for the Imam. By leaving Yemen they were making an independent decision and bringing back wealth to their families and village. Even today, when Yemenis return to their villages they are expected to put on feasts and share their wealth.

Abdullah Mohammed Saif said he was 75 years old.

'I went down to Aden, and lived there for about two years, or more. After going from Aden to Italy by ship, as a passenger, I went to London. I didn't speak English, I didn't know how to ask for water or the toilet.'

'I went to Birmingham to work in a factory,' continued Abdullah, 'and stayed there for a year or so and after that went to Swansea in south Wales, and stayed there for four to six months before going to sea, on the coal ships. I worked in the stoke-hole, cleaning the fire etc. It was the first time I took the coal from the bunker to the stoke-hole and from the stoke-hole into the fire. There were six holes and four hours of work to a shift. When you had bad weather you couldn't do anything about it. You must move the ship. You keep the coal in the fire, to keep the ship moving and get out of the area. I have been to America, Canada, Australia, Germany, Holland, Belgium, France and India – everywhere.'

Our arrival had unleashed a flood of memories from the past, and the history of Yemen's recent diaspora. Yemenis have ended up in all parts of the British Empire working on ships and even in mines and plantations. One stoker I spoke to had worked on British Rail steam trains as a fireman and I later met a British captain on a trip to Harris in the Outer Hebrides who told me that he remembered two Adenese seamen who worked in the engine room of the ferries in the Highlands and Islands of Scotland as late as the 1970s.

I looked at the seamen around me. They were fascinated by stoking and seemed content with their lives. There was a palpable sense of kinship, from their shared occupational history and backgrounds. They had travelled out of North Yemen at a time when the country was cut off from the outside world. Their spirit of camaraderie was one seen in all the old people gathered around us, but it had become more focused because of our presence in this place.

It was their time of exploration, their age of confidence. I could see them steaming up and down the Red Sea, through the Suez Canal, across the Mediterranean and around the British coast to the ports of Cardiff, Swansea, Newport, South Shields, Liverpool, London and Glasgow.

One old seaman quietly confessed to having married many

women, across the world during his long life at sea. It certainly was not unusual for those who settled in south Wales to take a Welsh wife and have at least one other at home in Yemen. One Yemeni in the early 1990s confessed to me to have left a wife at home in the 1940s and never returned, although this was unusual.

In fact, with such an extensive migration, much of the agricultural system back home relied on the women in the villages. Yemeni seamen, as it happens, sometimes took two names, almost changing their identity. It was as if they were taking on a new life, assuming an Adeni name before receiving their dispatch book and sailing out into the world. This caused some difficulties for the Arabs living in Britain later. Some were assumed to be aliens and not British subjects and there was much debate as to whether Yemenis from the highlands should be allowed the same status as Adenese.

Although not as tribal as highland Yemenis in the north, these men from the Shamir region did have many local loyalties. Changing your tribe is rare in Yemen and going to another tribe for help in some dispute with your own is very unusual. But these men were happy to leave for work on foreign ships to create a better standard of living for themselves and their families.

Mohammed Saif Kassem looked deeply into my eyes. He explained how as a stoker he had tried to feed the fire – keep it alive – the stoker might have water slopping about everywhere but dry coal was crucial. Even if water was pouring in through the funnel you would have to keep the fire burning. They would pump the water out, but it was never quite fast enough. Mohammed explained how they couldn't even eat properly, especially during the convoys of the Second World War, because it was so busy when the Germans were homing in on the convoys. The stoker was crucial to enable the ship to manoeuvre and many of the merchant ships that gave supplies to armies and civilians during the Second World War were quite old and built with early-twentieth-century technology.

I had to remind myself that these men sailed a very long time ago. I was trying to understand the pattern of things. They were tough and energetic, a dying breed, a testament to a courageous age. Abdo Ali Othman, a lecturer in the Department of Sociology at Sana'a

University and an expert on Yemeni migration, told me later that these men were extremely brave;

'They rarely spoke English, knew nothing of the outside world. The Imam told them that he ruled the earth, and anything he decreed they believed.'

It was as if salt water ran through their veins. From their fragments of conversation, which were gloriously vivid, I realised that a part of history which I thought had disappeared, was alive and well, and living on in the memories of these elderly men, from the midland belt of Yemen. Invisible, unknown travellers, hidden away in the engine-rooms of ships, in the same way miners had worked in the depths of the earth. In both cases, there was a deeply religious aspect to their work, Christian or Muslim. It was a responsibility to God and their family.

They also returned with money in their pockets. I thought of a Yemeni receptionist in London, whom I'd met some months previously who had said these men were 'slaves' as if their work had been some kind of incarceration but realised that there was far more to it than that. Particularly during the war when their expertise was justly rewarded.

On one John Cory & Sons ship the *Reading*, the crew register from 1883 lists a Mohammed Moosla, age 29, from 'Arabia' who was paid nine pounds two shillings and three pence for his duty. Another, Ali Mersa, age 24 from 'Aden' was paid eight pounds, sixteen shillings and seven pence, while a third, Omar Hassan, age 34 from 'Aden', who had boarded the ship later, received one pound and ten shillings.

Here in the midland belt they were now living out the peaceful remains of their life, in contentment, with good memories and a British pension.

The following year in Aden I learnt that there were even colloquial expressions about Cardiff in everyday Yemeni Arabic usage. Showki Bahumaid, head of English at Aden University, who had studied linguistics at Bangor University in north Wales and researched colloquial Adenese, introduced me to Mohammed Shukri, head of Islamic History at the University, who had relatives in Cardiff.

'We have a saying about people who throw their money about

carelessly,' he said. 'We say in Arabic, 'He didn't work hard for it in Cardiff.' It is a reference to the hard work the stokers did.' Another expression I heard from Suleiman Ghanem, a member of the Yemen Embassy staff in London, who grew up in Aden, was that if, as a child, he thought too much of himself, his father would turn to him and say 'don't think like this of yourself – you're not from Cardiff.' This comment reflects the reverential way in which Yemenis once saw their contemporaries who had travelled the world and returned comparatively affluent. In some villages near Taiz when two people are seen hugging each other in a friendly embrace, a third may say 'He must have just returned from Cardiff.'

Like their ancestors who had burned incense, they in their turn burned coal in the engine rooms of steamships, sending smoke up into the heavens. Their Southern Arabian ancestors had traversed the vast deserts with their camels to distribute incense for the altars of far away lands, where burnt offerings were needed to appease the gods and prepare and save the soul. I realised I was sitting with seafaring Bedouin of exceptional spirit and valour who had travelled the great oceans offering coal to the fire, and consigning their ashes to the sea. Many of these war-time Yemenis had gone down with their fires into the oceans' depths. It was their sacrifice. It was their burning ashes, it was their time.

The Welsh blanket, Taiz

The Welsh Blanket

'The past and future sit together as friends.'
(Yemeni proverb)

We were once again well away from the sounds of the main road, only the warm tones of the old Arab sailors stayed with us as we drove along the *wadi* with its never ending stream of livestock: bullocks, donkeys and goats. The atmosphere in the Landcruiser was pensive. Outside, tall palm trees provided a little shade for a man ploughing with his camel in the heat of the day. People congregated around a few small huts cooking on open fires. Pungent clouds of smoke floated towards mounds of fodder at the roadside. A nearby stream doubled as a play area for local children.

Everyone around us looked settled, but we were disorientated. Naji once again stopped to ask the way to the villages which we had been told in Hagdah were home to Yemenis from Britain. We had the good luck this time of finding a young man who recognised the name 'Cardiff.' He offered to travel with us and navigate us towards an area called Moqbana, where he told us there were people with relatives in Cardiff. It was perhaps the first time on our journey that travelling without a decent map failed to concern us. The young man hopped up on the running-board and clung to the outside of the vehicle. Our own personal guide, he knew every twist and turn we needed to take. I thought of Taha Muhammed's story of the *Tabal*, the messenger, with his donkey bank bringing money to the stokers families.

Finally we arrived in a beautiful valley of low gentle hills, with rocky outcrops, covered with green trees and neat houses. It was a paradise called Katina.

We drove to the nearest cluster of houses. A vehicle was leaving the hamlet in the opposite direction but it stopped and two men got out to greet us. One spoke perfect English and welcomed us with the warmth of the father of the prodigal son. He explained that he had spent much of his life working in Birmingham in a biscuit factory. He had been part of the second wave of migration into Britain, after the demise of the steamships, when Britain needed labour in its northern and midland industrial belts. Ahmed explained that we had been researching into the travels of old Arab seaman, who had worked with coal. They laughed.

'Britain stopped using coal ships after the Second World War! But all the old men in these villages worked on the ships.' said one of them. 'All of them, honestly you would not believe it. All of them.' He then paused and said. 'If you come from Cardiff then you must know Sheikh Said.'

Charles, Ahmed, Naji and I all looked at each other. It was a significant moment.

This was the first time someone had mentioned Sheikh Said without being prompted.

'Yes, we know Sheikh Said very well. How do you know him?' asked Charles.

'That is his house over there,' said the man pointing down through some fields.

We turned around, and through the haze we looked back down the valley. In the distance stood a solitary house, like a rare piece of sculpture, perched neatly on a platform of rock. Our spirits rose.

'*That* is the house of Sheikh Said?' I said.

'Yes.'

Ahmed murmured a few words in Arabic. 'I don't believe this,' he said. 'This is *too* much of a coincidence.'

All travel in some way is a pilgrimage. Instinct, intuition and trust are the pilgrims friends.

Travel, like art, gives us a place to go. Here we were standing in a remote village linked to those we knew – but who lived elsewhere.

'Go down there and you will find his wife, Wilaya and his son Ahmed living there.'

Naji drove down the hill with the enthusiasm of a man who had just been informed of the location of buried treasure.

Then Ahmed spoke. 'This is one of the most beautifully-painted houses I have ever seen, in the whole of Yemen.' The house was remarkable. Built of grey stone, with ultramarine shutters and decorated in the fluid designs of a minor master, creating drama and splendour. Nearby stood a small white beehive tomb which we were later to discover was the resting place of Sheikh Said's adoptive father, the one who had asked King George if he would like to become a Muslim.

As we arrived at the front of the house Ahmed turned to us and smiled 'Do you know anyone from Cardiff?'

He knocked on the front door and within a minute Wilaya was standing in front of us, in a long floral dress and neat coloured head scarf revealing jet black hair. I reached into my bag and brought out a photographic portrait of Sheikh Said that I had taken in Cardiff at the local mosque.

'Oh' she gasped, and held it to her breast, then showed it to her young son who had arrived at the door. Ahmed and she exchanged words in Arabic as her son, grinning, gripped the side of her dress, and kissed the picture of his father with affection.

'She says she is very happy to see you. She sent Sheikh Said a letter today, and asks you to tell him to phone her and send some clothes for his son.'

Wilaya stepped down and took my hand, and we exchanged greetings. After a few minutes she led me to a compound. Inside she opened a shed. Out came two handsome ginger cows, some sheep and chickens – valuable livestock. Wilaya smiled. Britain was well known here, and respected for the economic support it had given to so many local families.

'We were fishing for oysters, and we found a pearl', exclaimed Ahmed after our visit to Katina.

* * *

We awoke late in Taiz after a long drive the previous day, and were hungry for a breakfast of beans and fried lambs' livers. Sprawled around the foot of the 3,200 metre-high Jebel Sabr, Taiz, the country's second largest city, appeared to consist of endless acres of nondescript concrete housing, businesses and factories reminiscent of the British Midlands. In fact this area of Yemen is often called the Midland belt and many of its inhabitants have connections with the English cities of Birmingham and Sheffield. The visitor could be easily fooled into thinking that Taiz is an invention of the modern age but its history stretches back to pre-Islamic times and it has been the capital of Yemen on a number of occasions. It is warmer than Sana'a in the winter and cooler than Aden in the summer. Irrigation has produced some rich agricultural areas. As much as 25 inches of rain fall between April and October, so the variety of local foodstuffs in the market was impressive. Throughout the centuries, Taiz has been a gateway to the Highlands. When the Ottoman Turks arrived in Yemen in 1546, the city became a centre for military sorties into the interior and also acted as an administrative centre for goods arriving from Mocha and Aden.

It had a golden period between the thirteenth and fifteenth centuries when, under Rasulid control, it became an important centre of political power and trade. Much of the old city wall which dates back to this era has largely disappeared, although the two city gates still remain: the Bab Musa and the Bab Al Kabir. It is the mosques of this period that are the most important. The oldest, the Al-Muzaffar (c.1210-1370), with its 20 white cupolas, is the best surviving and visually the most interesting, while the Al-Ashrafiyah, is remarkable for its minarets and interior plaster decoration. The great dome of the northern prayer hall is one of the most magnificent artistic achievements in Yemen.

Although the centre of power in Yemen has moved from one place to another, it was only in the twentieth century under Imam Ahmed that Taiz became a capital again during his residency here following Imam Yahya's assassination in 1948. I had been determined to revisit Imam Ahmed's palace, now a museum, since we had arrived in Yemen, and we made our way through the busy streets to its large stone entrance.

Inside it had been left much as it was before the 1960s revolution. It was dark and gloomy. Old broken radios used by the Imam to listen to the BBC lay scattered on the floor. Beside these, 1950s film spools were stacked on a table next to which the guards chewed qat. Under a cascading chandelier, baroque style mirrors and gold framed pictures hung on the walls. Faded tapestries, unpolished silver jewellery and bric-a-brac of all kinds overflowed from cabinets. We stepped upstairs past a Persian carpet nailed to the wall and into a room packed with embroidered silk and cotton clothes. I needed to find the cupboard in which I had seen a brightly coloured Welsh blanket, back in 1983.

We wandered through the interconnecting rooms, trawling every wardrobe and cabinet as we went. In the last room we reached, bright light was streaming through the window. On the left-hand wall stood a solitary glass cupboard. I looked at the top shelf. There, in the cupboard surrounded by memorabilia, folded up, looking comfortable in its surroundings, was the Welsh woollen blanket resting undisturbed, like an ancient relic.

It was a traditional double weave, rare in Britain today, two cloths simultaneously woven one on top of the other to create two distinct reversible patterns. Each different but complementing each other. The weaver crossing threads and strands, interlacing and uniting, two distinct sets of fibres. This cloth had a background of indigo surmounted by blues, reds and white. This weave was originally produced all over Britain, but continued longest in Wales due to the isolation of its inland valleys, a treasured record of the past.

The Welsh woollen mills were always situated by flowing water, as the wool and cloth needed to be boiled, steamed and pressed to create an exceptional wear resistance. They also needed the power through waterwheels to soften the texture of the wool, which was rough to spin as Welsh mountain sheep lived in harsh, wild environments with an irregular diet. This blanket was from Trefriw Woollen Mill. I was sure, as I had photographed the cloth there a few years previously. I later checked and found out that it was a cloth sold by the Mill to the 'Welsh Rural Crafts' shop in the Royal Arcade in Cardiff between 1940 and 1960, known sometimes as the Caernarfon pattern.

Most importantly, the blankets were loved, given as wedding gifts and became part of a woman's dowry. For in Wales you were born under the blanket, had your first wedding night under the blanket, and you died under the blanket. In early Wales it was one of the greatest gifts you could give a person. 'Craft is Greater than Gold,' says the old Welsh proverb. How it had arrived here we will probably never know, but it must have come by sea.

Sheikh Said had suggested that it must have been brought to the Imam as a gift by a Yemeni, perhaps even his own father. In those days it would have taken weeks to travel by steamship to Aden and then a week travelling inland on remote mountain donkey tracks to reach Taiz. A Welsh blanket is a bulky piece of hand luggage. Sheikh Said had himself left Cardiff and undertaken this gruelling journey in 1948, when he was eighteen years of age, in a quest to learn Arabic.

While in Taiz his father took him to the palace, which was surrounded by guards. Welcomed inside, they waited to be announced before entering a large room. The stone floor was covered with beautiful eastern carpets and scattered cushions. Imam Ahmed, a large rotund man with great bulging dark eyes and a forked beard, was dressed in white. Heaps of papers and sacks of letters from his subjects, dignitaries and foreign diplomats were stacked around him. At that time no 'foreigner' was allowed to enter Yemen without obtaining his personal permission. About twenty scribes were busily reading the mail at the back of the room and handing it to Imam Ahmed for discussion.

Sheikh Said's father had instructed him to lower his head in the King's presence, and kiss his knee. Sheikh Said described how as he stepped forward, Imam Ahmed stretched out his hand to prevent him from bowing. With his eyes looking down, Sheikh Said lost his footing and was thrown off balance, toppling backwards, his hands flew freely through the air and knocked over an old clock.

Their eyes met, as a nearby scribe picked up the clock and placed it back.

'Who is this boy?' Asked the King.

'He is the son of the Sheikh who is visiting from Britain.'

The Imam looked at Sheikh Said and said, *'Mashallah, Mashallah'*
'What God wills.'